Blood, Sweat & Gears

Ramblings on
Motorcycling and Medicine

by flash gordon, m.d.
Fellow of the American College of Emergency Physicians

A Whirlaway Book
Whitehorse Press
North Conway, New Hampshire

A Whirlaway Book. Published July, 1995 by

   Whitehorse Press

   P.O. Box 60

   North Conway, New Hampshire 03860, U.S.A.

Whirlaway and Whitehorse Press are trademarks of Kennedy Associates.

ISBN 1-884313-03-5

5 4

Printed in the United States of America

Contents

Experience is the worst teacher. It always gives the test first and the instruction afterward.

Consider this book a crib sheet.

This is not a textbook on first aid. It's a collection of columns that originally appeared in CityBike, northern California's premiere motorcycling monthly. Most local references are to the San Francisco Bay area. Each column contains a medical "pearl" that sooner or later may come in handy.

Blood, Sweat & Gears is not intended to replace the care of a professional, but it can give you some perspective on a particular health problem. In some cases, you'll learn how to prevent problems from occurring, or how to do what's needed until you can see your health care pro. In most cases, knowing what to do first can save you unnecessary pain. It may even save you the time and expense of a doctor's visit.

In any case, knowledge is power.

And yes, flash *is* my real name: it's on the mortgage and my medical license. I'm residency trained and board certified in emergency medicine, and have practiced in Miami, Detroit, Boston, Las Vegas, and San Francisco. I've been the Director of the Emergency Residency Program at San Francisco General Hospital, a practicing emergency doc, and Medical Director of the Haight Ashbury Free Medical Clinic. I now work in San Rafael, California. My office is called First Med Marin.

I've been riding motorcycles since 1961, and currently ride a highly modified BMW R-Series Twin around San Francisco. My writing has appeared in

CityBike magazine, the Whole Earth Review, a number of nationally distributed motorcycle monthlies, and other publications.

If you've got access to the Internet, you can reach me at flash@well.com. Feel free to stop by http://www.well.com/user/flash—that's my home page.

"You should write something about passengers," said Blue, who's often on the back of my bike. "Riding with you was the first time in years I've been on a bike. I didn't realize there was so much to do and know. You could write your pointers and people could leave them around casually for their passengers to find . . . "

"That's a good idea," I replied.

I'd been sitting at the computer, the day after my CityBike deadline, without a clue about what to do for my next column. Her idea was sounding better and better. "You know, that's a damn fine idea. Damn fine."

I began to type . . .

OK, what are some health-related aspects of having a passenger?

First of all, if your passenger is new to motorcycling, don't assume he or she will dress sensibly. If you say you're gonna go on a run for say, a few hours, let her (OK, him or her, but I'm just gonna say "her" from now on) know that shorts and a T-shirt are probably not the right thing to wear.

All of us who ride have learned about "windchill factor"—but you'd be surprised how hard it is to convince someone that riding for 30 minutes in 50-degree weather will be more fun with the right clothes—for example, long johns. I personally feel that long johns are great between October and April for almost every activity not done horizontally.

Explain to your passenger the wonderful skin-preserving and wind-cutting qualities of leather. I

Passengers

Sensible dress

Leather

7

keep an old leather jacket or two around for my passengers—and though they look funky, they appreciate it at 60 mph. I also have a soft spot in my heart for women wearing leather.

Boots

Footwear's important, too. I've taken care of lots of feet injured in bike accidents. I don't feel comfortable when my passenger's wearing high heels or flip flops. Boots are good. Army boots are great! In fact, when my friend June showed up for the ride to the Grateful Dead show wearing paratrooper boots, it absolutely made my day. Of course, she doesn't have any kids who can be criticized for their mom's choice of footwear. ("Hey, kid. Your mother wears . . . oh, never mind!")

I love watching all the cute young things riding down Haight Street on their scooters, wearing leather jackets and tights. At least, I think they're wearing tights. It could be spray paint, for all I can tell. It protects about as much as spray paint would, too. Tell your passengers the facts of life. Of course, if you're the kinda guy who never wears a helmet and rides in sneakers and a T-shirt—hey, you deserve each other. Evolution in action, if you ask me.

Mounting/Dismounting

OK—now we're ready to ride. One thing I caution my passengers about—DON'T get on or off until I'm ready. I recall one occasion in a parking lot when the woman I was riding with decided to hop on the back without telling me. I was absorbed in a map at the time. She put one foot on the footpeg, and . . . well, at least she helped me pick up the bike. The rule of thumb I use is to ask the passenger to wait for a nod before getting on or off. A wink's as good as a nod, of course.

I also tell my passengers this: DON'T move around when the bike is stopped. This rule exists because I'm short (about the same height as Hitler, Mussolini, and Napoleon) and have a fairly tall seat. If you're on something that lets you put both feet flat on the ground, you don't need to worry as much. You can catch the bike more easily as it starts to tip after your passenger leans way over to check if she got mud on her shoe.

The last thing I tell passengers is that a bike is steered by weight transfer, not the handlebars. I let the passenger move around while I'm riding hands-off (in a safe place) to show her how much her motion affects the bike's direction. I warn her about moving around a lot in turns. In fact, Blue tells me that when we're leaning a lot, she likes to close her eyes to prevent her natural tendency to sit up straight. I haven't tried that myself—yet.

Stay Close

In select cases, I tell her how important it is that she be as close to me as possible. The two phrases that I've invented over the years that work well are "we have to consolidate the center of gravity" and "it's vital that you, me and the bike move as one." Most people believe this. It's probably true, too.

That's it. Remember—a warm, happy passenger is a lot more fun after the ride than a cold, terrified one, and she's much less likely to strangle you. That's a major health benefit right there!

There are too many new riders out there without helmets. You can always tell new riders by how they always leave their feet down for the first couple of seconds after they take off from a stop. I guess they expect the laws of physics not to work until they hit about 20 mph. My guess is that these folks are "profilers" who want to be sure everybody can see them and know who they are. Even some Beemer riders do it. I recently saw an accident in San Francisco. This one wasn't the rider's fault; a car pulled out right in front of him. He was only doing maybe 20 mph when his head hit the road. That's all it took to kill him. If he'd had a helmet on, he'd be alive. No question about it at all. Some folks say that helmets interfere with your ability to see and hear. I think that's true, but to such a minor extent that it isn't worth the needless vulnerability and loss of control. If you have a helmet on, you can concentrate more on the ride and less on worrying about keeping your delicate squash from getting smeared all over the front bumper of some near-sighted blue-haired lady's Buick.

Helmets

Life is a series of trade-offs. I know that my helmet (a BMW System 2) does restrict my vision significantly in the vertical direction, but I don't care if I miss an occasional Highway Patrol traffic plane. And it keeps the pigeon shit out of my hair, too. The System 2 helmet is interesting in that the whole front of the helmet is hinged. This lets you put it on like an open face, and then swing down the front assembly, chin bar, face shield and all. This not only makes it real handy for people who wear glasses, it

Field of Vision

also gets the face shield closer to your face. This makes the opening effectively a lot larger. Try making a face-shield-size opening with your hands and then moving in closer and farther from your eyes and see what happens to the edges. It increases your field of vision dramatically.

Torque

Having the face shield closer to your face helps a lot when riding at speed, too. The wind doesn't catch the front part of the helmet when your head is turned, so it doesn't torque your head around like it does in some helmets. Makes it easier to look back over your shoulder each time you change lanes, which is something that'll keep you alive. And staying alive is the name of the game.

TURBO RIDGES

SPOILER & RADAR DETECTOR

FOG-FREE SHIELD

HELMET

GROUND EFFECT NECK WARMER

What do you need in a first aid kit? That depends: Do you spend most of your time within the city limits, or do you find yourself riding down to Baja every fall?

If you're a city rider, just stick a few bandages and some antibiotic ointment in your tool kit. You'll always be within a few minutes of an emergency room.

If you do weekend rides out in the country, you need more than just Band-Aids. Check out the list below.

Long distance tourers will want to carry all of the items below. Don't forget your prescription meds, along with their original bottles. A copy of your glasses prescription is worthwhile anytime.

BAND-AIDS: Band-Aids are the brand of adhesive bandage sold by Johnson & Johnson. The best kind are the stretchy, elastic kind, since they bend with you and don't fall off immediately. Coverlet brand bandages come in a box of assorted shapes, including knuckle, fingertip and standard shape. Highly useful. Remember, though, that putting a bandage over a cut or scratch that hasn't been disinfected is like giving the germs a house to hang out in . . .

DISINFECTANT: Povidone iodine is the best. It doesn't sting like old-fashioned iodine or Mercurochrome, and works lots better. Betadine is the best known brand. Get an 8-oz. bottle and keep it at home in the kitchen, where you keep your first aid kit (What? You keep it in the bathroom? When was

First Aid Kits

Prescriptions

Adhesive Bandages

Disinfectant

the last time you got cut or burned in the bathroom?) and just carry a little 2-oz. bottle with you.

ELASTIC BANDAGES: Often called Ace wraps (a brand name), they're useful for wrapping sprains, immobilizing fractures along with a splint, holding ice packs on sore areas, and for bondage. No, just joking. I wanted to see if anybody has read this far . . . A 3-inch band is the most useful size (good for wrists) but, if you have room, take a 6-inch, too (for knees).

Elastic Bandages

GAUZE PADS: It's worth carrying a few 2" x 2" and some 4" x 4" gauze pads (called "two by twos" and "four by fours" in the med biz — just don't try to buy 'em in a lumber yard . . .) for use in covering burns, scrapes, cuts and nicks, and for use in cleaning injuries. You just pour some disinfectant on a gauze pad and swab out the wound. Scream if you like. Better yet, have a friend with sadistic tendencies help.

Dressings

NON-STICK GAUZE: Best known brand is the Telfa pad. Use 'em on areas of road rash, so removing the pad won't cause you to use language you wouldn't want your mom to hear . . . Remember, in using any kind of gauze or dressing, DON'T TOUCH THE PART THAT IS GOING TO TOUCH THE WOUND!! Your fingers will contaminate it, and so much for cleaning it out in the first place.

GOOP: Actually, antibiotic ointment. Triple antibiotic ointment, Neosporin, Bacitracin; all are just about as good. Get whatever's cheapest, and wrap it in something so the vibration from your bike doesn't rub a hole in the side and cause it to leak all over the place. You don't need a sterile spark plug wrench . . .

Ointment

WIRE SPLINT: A useful item to have if you'll be spending time in the boonies. It's a piece of heavy-duty chicken wire that you can fold into a splint and wrap with an elastic bandage to use for fractures. If you or a rider have to ride with a fracture, a good splint is good news.

Splints

TRIANGULAR BANDAGE: Just a big piece of cloth. Useful for slings and for bandaging different areas. They were standard issue during wartime, and, considering the attitudes some people have while riding in their cars on freeways, maybe not inappropriate now. Don't forget the safety pins for this.

Zinc Oxide

ZINC OXIDE: Good for healing scrapes and burns. Helps 'em dry out and heal faster. Start using it about the second day—use "goop" (see above) the first day.

First Aid Course

Together, all of the above weigh about half a pound, and fit into an area the size of a paperback book. You can call your local American Red Cross chapter to find out about a first aid course , if you're going more than a couple of hours away from "civilization." Of course, people's definitions of civilization vary quite a bit. For me, it's not civilized if I can't get a pizza delivered at midnight seven days a week . . .

Road Rash

Pavement dermatitis (also known as "road rash") affects us all, sooner or later. Preventing it is easier than curing it—and good leathers, gloves, and shoes help do the trick. Every time I see somebody on a scooter wearing shorts, or a black leather jacket and black tights, I cringe. Road rash can be a pain in the . . . well, a pain wherever on the body it occurs.

Road Rash Prevention

The first step in treating road rash is plenty of running water and soap. The sooner after injury you do this, the better. Half an hour makes a BIG difference. If you can stop and use a gas station bathroom to wash, so much the better. If you find that washing is painful, a good trick is to rub the area with an ice cube for about five minutes until it gets numb. Don't try to get the dirt out until AFTER you've washed with soap and water. Otherwise you'll just be pushing germs into your body. If you find this still too painful, find a sadistic friend to do it to you. If you can't numb it with ice, have your friend use earplugs. This would be a good time to apply an antibiotic solution such as Betadine (the chemical name is povidone iodine) to kill germs. You can buy it in a drugstore, and a 2-oz. squirt bottle of it would be helpful in your first aid kit.

Treatment

The important thing is to get all the little ground-in pieces of dirt and rock and asphalt and whatever out of your skin. If you leave them there, they'll stay forever. This process is called "tattooing." The best way to get 'em out is with a sharp sterile needle or pin. If you stick the dull end of a needle into a cork or into a pencil eraser, it'll have a handle you or your

Pick Dirt Out

accomplice can hold on to. You must get EVERY LITTLE PIECE OUT! This is important. If you can still see it now, you'll always see it. If you can't get it all out, go to your doctor that day or to an emergency room. We're used to dealing with road rash, and can sometimes let it soak with a 4% Xylocaine solution for ten minutes or so, which numbs the skin.

Antibiotics

After digging out all you can see, numb it up again with the ice and wash it again. Apply some more Betadine, if you have it, and then put on some goop (antibiotic ointment) starting the second day. I like to use zinc oxide ointment—it's cheap, easily available (it's the same stuff surfers smear on their noses to prevent sunburn) and tends to help wounds dry up and heal faster. Put on a good thick layer of the zinc oxide.

Dressing

The next step is a dressing, or bandage. This just keeps germs and dirt out while giving your skin a chance to heal. I'd recommend a Telfa pad, if you have one, since they won't become part of the scab and won't cause you to use colorful language when you change the dressing on the second day.

Dressing changes should be every day, starting the second day. The least painful way to get the dressing off, if you didn't use a Telfa pad, is to soak it off. Just take warm water with a little hydrogen peroxide (to help loosen the dried blood) and soak the wound and the dressing that sticks to it. Take as much of the dressing off as you can before soaking. Next, use some ice again (one trick is to freeze a Styrofoam cup full of water and peel off a half inch of Styrofoam each time. Then you can rub the scrape with the ice and use the cup as a handle) to numb it and then take a wash cloth and soap and water and wash off all the gooey pus and stuff. If it bleeds a little, no problem. Then apply the zinc oxide, redress it, and repeat this daily 'til the new skin is there, all dry and pink.

Sunburn

One tip: new skin that's pink will sunburn and turn dark VERY easily. I recommend you use a #15 (or higher) sunblock (which you can buy in any drugstore) for a few months on the new pink area, until it matches the rest of your tan.

18

One more tip: Make sure you've had a tetanus shot within five years of any injury that breaks the skin. It's important. I remember complaining to the nurse when I was a kid getting a tetanus booster, saying,

"Hey, what did people do before they invented tetanus shots?"

She looked at me with a grin like you'd see on a shark.

"They died," she said . . . and gave me the shot.

Roasting the Fatted Calf

An attractive young woman Roast Calf
(whose name, sadly, I can't recall) came to see me at
the Haight Ashbury Free Medical Clinic. She was
suffering from the scourge of all motorcycle riders
who wear shorts: the classic "roast calf."

The "roast calf" has nothing in common with the Cause
old Wild West custom of taking a calf, spitting it, and
roasting it over a fire. It occurs when an innocent
person decides to go riding their bike wearing less
than full leg protection. "Less than full" includes leo-
tards or stockings, as I've noticed on Haight Street.
Well, actually, I've done more than just "notice"—in
some instances I've studied the situation intently.
Purely for scientific reasons, you understand.

Typically, the victim is a young woman, though
guys are also dumb enough to wear shorts on a bike.
The injury is usually about as big across as the muf-
fler. Folks usually come in after two or three days,
once the wound's already infected. This is a Bad
Thing To Do. If the burn is taken care of initially, it
heals faster with less chance of scarring.

The initial treatment, once all the cursing and Treatment
screaming is over, is cleaning and disinfecting the
burn. If you have the little bottle of Betadine mentioned on page 13 in the chapter on first aid kits, use
it now. Pour some on a piece of sterile gauze (which
should also be in the kit) and wipe it all over the
burn. Next, apply some antibiotic ointment to the
burn, cover it with a piece of sterile gauze, bandage
it, and then clean it every day, as described below.

Next, find a bathroom and wash the burn with Blisters
soap and water. If you've already got a blister that's

popped, you should remove the roof of the blister. The way I'd do it would be to hold up the middle of the blister with tweezers while clipping around the edge with sharp sterile scissors. If you don't have sterile scissors, soak some in the Betadine solution first, or in alcohol. Don't let the alcohol get into the burn, though, unless you *really* like pain. Cutting through skin that's part of the roof of a blister is painless—the nerves aren't connected anymore.

If the blister is still intact, and not leaking at all, gently wash it and the skin around it with soap and water, and follow that with some Betadine, antibiotic ointment, and a sterile dressing. Even though it's intact now, it's a good idea to get the area clean for when it does pop—you don't want germs getting inside there and causing an infection.

Charring

If the skin is charred all the way through, and you can't feel anything, you've got a third degree burn. This is worth taking to the hospital emergency room (along with a good novel to read during the wait) and having checked. Sometimes skin grafts are needed for third degree burns. You should still treat them initially as above, with cleansing and antibiotic ointment and a dressing.

Changing Dressings

Now, imagine it's not a third degree burn, and it's the next day: time to change the dressing. After removal, hopefully all you'll see is a nice clean burn with no redness around the edges or pus that indicates an infection. In that case, liberally apply the zinc oxide, and put on another sterile dressing. Remember, nothing should touch the part of the dressing that's going to be against the burn. Change the dressing daily and it should heal in a couple of weeks. Watch for redness, swelling, increasing pain or tenderness, red streaks going up your leg, or pus. These are signs of infection that might need antibiotics.

In Case of Infection

If the burn does get infected, you'll know it. Instead of being clean and healthy looking, you'll see pus when you remove the bandage. If so, you have to clean all the pus off. To do this with a minimum of pain, use the "ice in a Styrofoam cup" method described on page 18, and hold it against the burn for a few minutes. This acts like the ice cube folks use to numb ears before piercing 'em, and works well. Once it's numb, take a washcloth with COLD water and gently clean away the pus and dead skin. You can use the ice again if you want to. Then, clean with the Betadine again and apply zinc oxide. After the first day or so of antibiotic ointment, I like to use zinc oxide to help healing.

Don't forget that burns need tetanus shots, just like puncture wounds. ANY broken skin is an invitation to tetanus, it's not just the rusty nail. If it's been more than five years since your last tetanus booster, you need another one.

Tetanus

Poison Oak

Summer weather isn't too bad for riding, but it's lousy for trees. If you're a tree, you get brown and thirsty in a sunny summer. Luckily, very few trees read what I write so I don't anticipate any flack about this. In fact, I've noticed that most trees tend to avoid reading books and newspapers altogether. Maybe it has something to do with the fact that newsprint is made from trees, and they boycott 'em. Hmm, we may be on to something here—the chlorophyll conspiracy.

Come to think of it, trees don't like motorcycles much, either. What have they ever given to motorcycling? Scenery, sure, but I'm talking *real* contributions—you ever see a wooden bike? Me neither. Don't get me wrong—I think the woods are beautiful. I just wouldn't want to live there. Of course, I've camped out, some. It's fun, for a while. So's riding a roller coaster, but I wouldn't want to ride one 24 hours a day. I'm not talking about living in a nice *house* in the woods—I'm talking about living down there in a tent with the dirt and the bugs and the poison oak.

Now, there are some real guerrillas in the war between man and the plant world: poison oak, poison ivy and poison sumac. They're all over. Next time you find yourself out in the woods, ask somebody who used to be a Boy or Girl Scout to point some out to you. They work by secreting an oil that causes an allergic reaction in a lot of people. It takes a couple of hours for the oil to work, so if you know you've been exposed, wash your skin off with soap and water or try a moist towelette like they sell in plastic boxes

Trees

Wash it Off

for baby's bums. That'll remove most of it. Don't forget to wash other things that might have touched the plants—like shoes, backpacks, and dogs. They can carry the oil for quite a while. There've been cases of folks getting reactions after touching objects that have been locked away for thirty years—so make sure you get the oil off. A plain wet rag will take care of it. Wear rubber gloves when you do it.

Symptoms

How do you know when you've got it? I see folks about four to five days after exposure—they probably itched a day or so before that. The rash is on the parts of the body that get exposed to the plant—usually arms, but sometimes legs, for those folks unlucky enough to have been wearing shorts while communing with nature. The rash is a series of little blisters on red skin. It itches. The blisters are often in a line—and if you imagine the oil being wiped off a branch onto your skin, you'll understand the pattern. You get the blisters wherever the plant touches you.

Treatment

We usually treat it with a topical steroid. Hydrocortisone ½% is available in the drugstore. It's usually not strong enough, though. There are stronger creams and ointments available on prescription such as Kenalog, but I prefer using steroid pills called prednisone for a short course for a good case of it. I give folks the 20mg tablets, three a day for three days, two a day for three days, and then finish with one a day for three days. That usually knocks it out. Steroid shots work, too.

Infection

You have to watch for skin infections that come from scratching. If the rash gets red and warm, and has a yellowish crust on it, it's probably infected. Your doc'll probably give you an antibiotic to take if that happens—otherwise, the infection will keep it from healing.

Unbelievable But True

I once had a couple come in to see me in the E.R. who'd been overcome by passion while out in the boonies and didn't have a blanket. "Let's make a pile of these little plants," he suggested. Wrong. They had poison oak everywhere you could imagine, and some places you couldn't. I told 'em the pills would knock out all the itching in a day or so.

"Great!" said the guy; but the woman didn't seem happy.

"What's wrong?" I asked.

"Is there something you can give me that won't stop all the itching?" she asked. "It feels good in one particular place." This is the truth.

I told her that a case as bad as hers needed the pills—the cream just wouldn't do it. The last I saw of 'em they were walking out of the E.R., hand in hand. I guess they had some scratching to do while they could . . .

Scratch

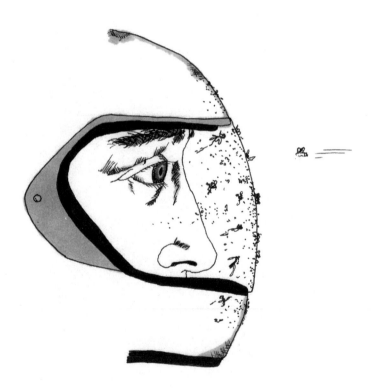

Here's Lookin' at You, Kid

What's the most sensitive part of your body? Fingertips? Go ahead, rub two fingertips together. Did that hurt? No? What else is sensitive? Well, don't start rubbing THAT in public . . . Beyond a doubt, the most sensitive part of your body is the clear, front part of your eye, called the cornea. We all know what a piece of dust in our eye, or an accidental scrape, can feel like.

Guess What? Eyes

A piece of dust weighs maybe a thousandth of a gram. A person weighs about seventy million times as much. Despite your weight advantage, that dust can be as lethal as a semi coming into your lane on a blind curve—if that dust makes you blink at the wrong time.

Dust Motes in Thine Eye

Good goggles help; so do helmet face shields. Winnebago-style riders have windscreens. Sometimes that's not enough. Here's how to deal with something in your eye, known medically as a foreign body (which has nothing to do with Sonia Braga).

Prevention

First, don't wait to get it out. You might think, "Gee, I'll be home in ten minutes—I'll get it then." No good. The clear part of the eye (the cornea) is relatively soft in front—at least as compared to dust or sand. When you blink, you drive that piece of dust in deeper and deeper (if blinking doesn't knock it loose, as it's supposed to). In a few minutes, it can be deep in the cornea where you won't be able to get it out yourself without scraping your eye.

Don't Wait

Be careful trying to wipe it out with the wet corner of a handkerchief, which some first aid books recommend. Just touching the cornea will scrape it,

Careful!

29

and it will hurt like hell and take longer to heal. Here's one method to get out just the dirt.

Treatment

Grab the eyelashes and pull the eyelid straight forward away from the eyeball. While holding the eyelid out, look UP (or have the victim look up) as high as possible. Then pull the eyelid down as far as it will go, and lay it against the lower lid. While holding it there, look DOWN. Release the eyelid; blink a few times and, if you got to it soon enough, that should do the trick.

Metal Injuries

Another dangerous eye injury can occur when you're working with metal, and a piece of it hits your eye at high speed. This happens when metal hits metal, or if you use a grinder or other power tool without eye protection. If the metal penetrates the cornea and goes into your eyeball, it must be removed surgically.

Don't Wait #2

If not promptly removed (and sometimes even if it is), that eye may go blind. Then, occasionally, your remaining eye goes blind. Again, this only happens if a piece of metal is driven INSIDE your eyeball—not the typical situation, but one worth thinking about before trying to pound loose a nut without goggles. One tip—a helmet visor works likes goggles.

An interesting thing happens to pieces of iron and steel that get embedded in your cornea—unless taken out right away, they rust. That ring of rust around the speck of metal (known in medical terms, logically enough, as a "rust ring") can tattoo the clear part of the cornea you use to look through, damaging your vision. So, if something stays in your eye more than a few hours, get it checked.

Dirt Under Lid

Another eye problem that will quickly get you to your doc is something caught up under your eyelid. This will scratch your eyeball every time you blink, and it hurts like hell. If you think that this might be happening, you need to turn the eyelid inside out to look under it. It's more easily done on somebody else.

Treatment

First, take something like the tip of a pen or pencil, or a key, or anything small and dull, and put it against the top part of the eyelid. Then ask the victim to look down, and fold the lid back over the pencil tip. There's a semi-rigid plate in the bottom half of your lid that you can flip over whatever you're using that will stay up and let you inspect the bottom of the upper lid, preferably with good light, and, if you can get it, magnification. A piece of grit here can often be wiped away with a Q-tip or the wet corner of a tissue.

If you hurt your cornea, get it checked. The doc will probably patch it after taking out what's bothering you and checking for other damage. The doc will numb it; check your vision before and after; put some stuff in it to make injured parts of the cornea show up; remove the foreign body; put in a drop of antibiotic solution and maybe a drop to relax the muscle around the pupil to prevent cramps and pain; and, most importantly, put on a tight patch to encourage healing.

Healing and Patches

Most corneal scrapes and superficial injuries heal in one or two days. Taking ibuprofen is usually enough for the pain of a minor scrape. If you took a real good swipe or scratched your eye up a lot, it won't hurt to ask the doc for something stronger. Last—don't even THINK of riding your bike home with a patched eye. You'll have no depth perception and will most likely end up in the hospital.

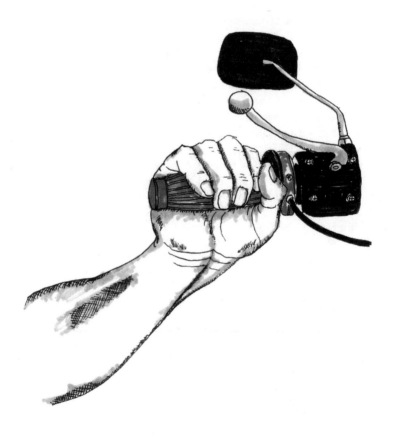

No Wrist for the Weary

I get lots of questions about carpal tunnel syndrome. It can be a real problem for bikers; improper hand position could cause or aggravate it.

Carpal Tunnel Syndrome?

What's the carpal tunnel? It's NOT a secret way for folks sharing rides into San Francisco to get under the bay. That would be the "car-pool tunnel." Actually, it's an area in your wrist that nerves and tendons to your hands pass through. There's not a lot of clearance through it, and swelling in this area can put pressure on the nerves and can cause numbness and pain, which may become permanent.

Causes

Repetitive trauma is a major cause of carpal tunnel syndrome. Classically, people like jackhammer operators get it, but now folks who do such things as computer keyboarding are showing up with it. Bikers are at risk if they ride with their wrists bent back. This squeezes the structures in the carpal tunnel, and can lead to carpal tunnel syndrome.

Symptoms

The most common symptoms of carpal tunnel syndrome are pain, numbness, and loss of feeling in the hand. The area served by the median nerve, which passes through the carpal tunnel, is mostly involved. People often complain of pains shooting up the arm from the wrist, especially at night, and can even develop weakness in the hand. Sometimes, folks first notice they have it when they start to drop things. In more advanced stages, it becomes difficult to make a fist.

How does carpal tunnel syndrome start? Inflammation and swelling of the tendon sheaths that go through the carpal tunnel, like you get in tendinitis, can cause the first episode. Wrist injury, such as a sprain, fracture, or dislocation, can also lead to carpal tunnel syndrome. If you've injured your wrist recently and are wearing a splint, cast, or even an elastic bandage, watch out for numbness or throbbing. If they occur, and elevation doesn't make them completely better, get in touch with whoever's taking care of you as soon as possible. Don't wait until the next morning—do it NOW.

Treatment

Treatment for carpal tunnel syndrome can be a long, drawn-out affair. There are two types of therapy: non-surgical and surgical. Non-surgical treatment includes aspirin, ibuprofen, or other non-steroidal anti-inflammatory drugs (conveniently known as NSAIDS) as well as rest, elimination of the precipitating cause, and often wrist splints. The splints seem to be very helpful for some patients. If you have carpal tunnel syndrome and haven't tried them, you should. Remember, also, that acetaminophen (as in Tylenol) doesn't have any anti-inflammatory effects, and shouldn't be used for the inflammation you'd have in tendinitis, bursitis, or arthritis. "Itis" is medical-ese for "inflammation," in case you were wondering.

Prevention

It's helpful to visualize what's going on and what can make it worse. Try this exercise:

Put your thumb on your wrist, right between the skin creases in the middle. Hold your wrist so it's straight out—not bent either backwards or forwards. Notice how the skin, tissues, and so on are loose when you press on them.

Now, bend your wrist back. Feel how tight and hard your wrist gets? If it's tight, it's squeezing the nerve. This is what you're trying to avoid.

Try to be aware of the position of your wrist. As you can imagine, if the carpal tunnel area is already swollen from tendinitis or arthritis, it'll be even tighter with your wrist back. Keeping your wrist in a neutral position is one of the big advantages of splints.

Surgery

Surgery for carpal tunnel syndrome shouldn't be done until you've tried more conservative measures, unless you've got an acute buildup of pressure due to trauma. If your symptoms are not being controlled or are getting worse with conservative measures, you might consider surgery. In any case, get a second opinion before surgery.

Who's the best doc to operate on a carpal tunnel syndrome problem? Try to find a doc who does lots of hand surgery. Your primary health care delivery person should be able to give you a hand.

So to speak . . .

Nerves of Jell-O

You'd be totally in the dark without your nerves. They carry all the information about what's going on outside your body to your brain, and also carry all control messages from the brain to the rest of the body. Think of 'em as phone lines, carrying information.

Nerves

I'm sure all of us have had an arm or leg "fall asleep." That's what happens when we compress the nerve going to that area for a while. Since the nerve uses chemical reactions to carry messages, squeezing an area of nerve for a while will cause it to stop functioning. The "pins and needles" sensation you feel is your nervous system's equivalent of static: i.e., what you hear when you tune an AM radio to an area between stations.

Pins and Needles

A pinched nerve can also give a painful sensation in the area being affected. Have you ever whacked your "funny bone"? That's the ulnar nerve where it passes through the elbow. You can get that sensation from pinched nerves, too. Typically, pinched nerves cause numbness, tingling or pain in the area served by the nerve. This can be quite a ways away from the area of injury: i.e., you can pinch a nerve in your neck and feel it in your arm and hand.

Pinched Nerves

Usually the nerve "wakes up" after a few minutes, and things are fine. Sometimes, though, if the pressure has been there for quite a while (hours) it will damage that section of nerve: i.e., it won't come back in a few minutes, as it will if it's just been compressed.

The most common example of the less temporary kind of injury is what's called "honeymoon paraly-

Honeymoon Paralysis

sis" (for those of you with your minds in the gutter, it's usually the person's ARM that's paralyzed). Typically, a couple goes to sleep after a significant quantity of alcohol or other central nervous system depressants, and the person whose arm is being slept upon doesn't want to wake up their partner. The next morning, their hand is partly numb and the victim can't extend the hand at the wrist.

When this happens, the nerve may have to re-grow itself from the point of injury. If the outside of the nerve hasn't been damaged, it'll usually regrow at the rate of one inch per month. So, if it's damaged 18 inches up the arm, it'll take a year and a half to recover completely. Sometimes it's faster, but at the end of that period, all the healing that's going to happen has happened.

Folks also get honeymoon paralysis when they pass out from drinking too much or taking stuff that knocks 'em out, and they fall asleep on their OWN arm. The picture and the prognosis is the same.

Syndromes of the Tunnels

Another form of pinched nerve can occur when-ever there's constant pressure on a nerve. The best known of these is carpal tunnel syndrome, which is covered in the previous chapter. In that condition, the median nerve gets squeezed in a tunnel going between the carpal bones in the wrist. Nerves can also be caught between bony prominences (as occurs in the neck) or squeezed between the bones in the ankles (so-called tarsal tunnel syndrome: the ankle bones are the tarsals; the wrist bones are the carpals).

Injuries

Sometimes nerves are injured when they get banged hard. After a tough get-off, for example, you might have a small area that's numb for a while. If you do notice any numbness or weakness after an accident, it's important to have a qualified health professional check you out. I've had people walk into my emergency room days after an accident who have had BROKEN NECKS and not known it.

Treatments

There are a few specific treatments for pinched nerves. In carpal tunnel syndrome, for example, if rest and splinting don't fix it up, the pressure can be relieved by surgery. Usually, though, there are no specific remedies: you just wait it out and protect the affected hand or foot by splinting if needed. Splinting will keep the soft tissues from deformation and contracture.

One last thought about nerves: your spinal cord and brain have about the same strength as does a bowl of Jell-O. Researchers have done x-ray movies of dog brains; you can see the brains quiver for a while after a head impact. That quivering tears up blood vessels in the brain, and causes the equivalent of a stroke in that area. Plus, the skull has several sharp areas in it that can literally tear the brain apart. You can hit your head hard enough to kill yourself by toppling off a bike at rest and hitting a curb.

Jell-O Brains

However, if you're one of the folks I see profiling themselves down Haight Street with your helmet on your elbow, think of this: you won't have to worry about feeling a pinched nerve in your ELBOW after an accident.

Real Jell-O Brains

It's the day after a long, hard ride. **Soreness**
You're not used to it, and you might be a little out of
shape. Your body reminds you of this fact when you
start to get out of bed.

What makes you sore after some kinds of physical activity? How do you treat it? How do you prevent it? First, you have to understand a little about
how the human body is put together.

Unlike most parts of a motorcycle, the tissues of
the human body have the ability to stretch without
breaking. Enough force, of course, can lead to a tendon or ligament giving way completely—and when
this happens, you're in for a significant amount of
down time. You can get overuse injuries from repetitive trauma (for example, see the chapter on carpal
tunnel syndrome), acute injuries that hurt muscles
or tendons (strains) or injuries that damage ligaments holding joints together (sprains).

Muscle strains occur when you've torn some of **Strains**
the microscopic fibers that make up the muscle itself. Tearing muscle fibers is normal during vigorous
exercise: in fact, you only build muscle by first
breaking it down through work. That's why you'll
feel sore after a vigorous workout sometimes; you're
feeling the microscopic tears in the muscle.

Sometimes, after a particularly hard workout,
you can see little bluish discolorations under the
skin. These are spots of bleeding from muscle damage.

One thing that's helpful in preventing muscle **Prevention**
strains is warming up before using that group of **Stretching**
muscles. Stretches are particularly good, especially

before vigorous activity. If all of a muscle's fibers are stretched, they're less likely to tear with exercise.

The kind of stretching you do depends on the activity you're anticipating. If you're going to be sitting on the seat of your Gold Wing and not moving for several hours, the stretches will be different than if you plan on racing dirt track. One point: sitting still for several hours can be more hazardous to your health than exercising. You run the risk of getting blood clots in your legs (called thrombophlebitis) if you sit too long without moving. I try to stop at least once an hour for five minutes or so and walk around, making sure I have good circulation in my legs, before continuing.

Treatment

If you do get injured and either strain a muscle or sprain a joint, be sure to "ice" it first (icing is most effective within 24 hours, but helps up to 48 hours later). Save the hot soaks for later. Icing an injured area will reduce the blood flow and the consequent bleeding into the area which is made worse by heat. Just think of what happens to your hands when you put them in hot water: they turn red. That red is just extra blood flow. You don't want that in a freshly injured area. Use cold instead. Imagine how your hands would look after being soaked in ice water: they'd be pale, right? That's from the decrease in blood flow from the cold.

Aspirin Warning!

Another hot tip: If you know you're going to be doing something that's likely to be leaving you tired and achy, take aspirin, ibuprofen, or Naproxen (not Tylenol) first. This can help prevent inflammation at the muscle level. If you wake up achy, take more aspirin. Adults can safely take two adult aspirin every four hours if needed for pain. Remember, when taking aspirin make sure that they don't smell like vinegar (otherwise they'll mess up your stomach) and that you take them with a full glass of water. They can, in some cases, eat a hole right into the stomach lining. OUCH!!

That's worth repeating: make sure that the aspirin you buy don't smell strongly like vinegar. If they do, they've gone bad. Return them if you just bought them, or toss them if they're old. But don't take them.

Last, and most important—try to stay in shape for your activities. If you plan on a strenuous activity, get in shape for it! Spend as little as thirty minutes three times a week getting and staying in condition. Your body will be grateful.

Stay in Shape

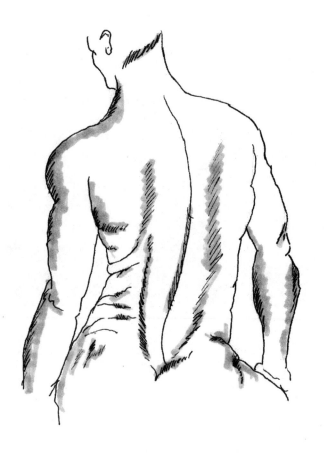

Get Back

A friend suggested I write about backs.

"My boyfriend's got a stiff one every morning when he gets up," she said.

I raised my eyebrows.

"His BACK is stiff," she said.

"Oh."

Why Backs Ache

Her SPOAS (what's SPOAS? Significant Person Of the Appropriate Sex) got a K75S in August. About three weeks later, his back started to hurt. That fits. An activity which involves new muscle groups often leads to stiffness or pain. In this case, going from rarely riding to over a thousand miles a month probably did it. He uses an aggressive riding position, leaning far forward (at least when she's with him on the freeway.) She also tends to lean up against him most of the time. I admit it's nice to have a SPOAS leaning up against you when you ride. You have to realize, though, that their weight bears directly on your lower back and arms, and can get tiring after a while. It can even lead to back problems.

Strains

Your back will let you know in one of two ways when it's not happy. The first way is for it to be stiff and achy, but still allowing you to be up and around. The pain is more dull than sharp, and you're not stuck in one position. This is often only a muscle strain, and can be helped a lot with a pain killer like aspirin, ibuprofen, or Naproxen—and massage.

Spasms

The other common way your back can get back at you (so to speak) for mistreating it is to have a muscle spasm. A muscle spasm in the back is just like a charley horse in your calf, except in size and location. It can be just as sudden, painful and disabling as a charley horse, too. When you get a cramp in your calf, you stretch it and massage it to get the circulation going again. Think of a back spasm the same way. It's tough to stretch, but you can help it with massage, as you can a back muscle strain.

Massage

For massage to be effective, the massagee has to be warm, comfortable, and relaxed. Though there are special chairs that will allow you to get a backrub while sitting, most people say it's better to be horizontal. I'm prone to agree. For "Swedish" style massage, the body should be bare from at least the waist up and you should lie face down on a comfortable surface. The room should be comfortably warm; shivering tenses muscles, and defeats the whole purpose. Since the goal of a massage (at least one of the goals) is to relax tight muscles, you should try to have the room quiet, perhaps with very quiet music.

It's important to know where the muscle spasms are in order to get 'em. To find the tight areas, you can first ask the backrubbee where it hurts. That should get you to the general area. To find the specific spot that's tight, just start massaging, and feeling for tight or hard areas. With a little practice, you should be able to tell where the tight spots are in no time at all.

Next, take some oil (massage oil works best, but you can use mineral oil or baby oil; please, not Redline or Castrol) and pour it into your hand to warm it up. DON'T pour it onto the back directly—it's cold and will cause the backrubbee to tense up, and that's what we're trying to avoid. It's also helpful to keep contact with the backrubbee by keeping the back of one hand on their back while you pour oil with the other.

Rub the oil over your finger tips, and then start rubbing with your thumbs on the backrubbee's shoulders. If you put your hands on their shoulders with your index fingers against their neck, you'll find your thumbs fall in an area that's often tense. Start there, rubbing moderately firmly in a circular motion. Ask the backrubbee to tell you if it should be harder or softer. After rubbing this area for a minute or two, you should feel the area getting softer. About this time the backrubbee will say "Ahhhh . . . ."

The next areas to rub and check are the muscles that parallel the spine, called the paraspinal muscles. They're about two inches to three inches apart on either side of the backbone. Never rub on the bones of the back; they can be tender. To get the paraspinal muscles, get some more oil (and it helps to keep the oil at hand) and warm it in your hand again. Start rubbing some oil on the paraspinals. If the backrubbee is very muscular, you might need to rub with the heels of your hands, or even your elbows. It often takes a lot of pressure to loosen up these muscles. When you find the area that's tight, just work on it. If you continue to rub it slowly and forcefully, it'll gradually relax.

Other Treatment for Backs

After having a mild back strain, you can usually get around OK, but should avoid heavy lifting for a few days, as well as sports involving sudden, unexpected motions, like football or basketball. Swimming would probably be alright. Back spasms, though, often necessitate bed rest for a day or so. Be sure to take aspirin, ibuprofen, or Naproxen. Hot baths can be helpful, as can ice rubs. Experiment to find out what works best for you. If it doesn't get better in a couple of days, see your chiropractor, bodyworker, or physician. And while you're resting in bed, you might want to read one of the many good books written on back care.

Danger Sign

IMPORTANT: If you get pain, numbness, or weakness in either leg, let your doctor know about it right away. This can be a symptom of a disc problem in your back. Pain shooting down a leg is called sciatica.

Stick It In Your Ear

Noise. There's lots of it out there. We live in a world full of noise, and, as motorcyclists, we make some of it ourselves. I'm not going to debate whether bikes are worth the noise they make: obviously, since a bike is my primary means of transport, I think it's worthwhile. But I'd like to tell you something pretty interesting I learned recently.

Noise

I helped start an organization called H.E.A.R., which is an acronym for Hearing Education and Awareness for Rockers (415 441-9081). It's a non-profit organization concerned with hearing and rock musicians—a lot of whom have lost hearing. We're trying to help destigmatize hearing loss, help get hearing aids to folks who need them, provide free hearing tests, and tell people about earplugs. What I found out about earplugs is what's interesting.

Hearing Problems

Briefly, earplugs help you hear better. This sounds strange, I know. What they do is cut the sound level down to where your ears can deal with it without distortion. It's like wearing sunglasses in bright light—they cut things down to where you can see better. Same with earplugs.

Earplugs

I've been using plugs on long rides, since the combination of bike noise and wind noise gets to me after a while. The plugs I use are the soft ones, made by a company called E-A-R.

By rolling them up real tight and letting them re-expand within your ear canal, they're comfortable and can give you about a 30 db reduction in noise. That's a lot. What it does for me on rides of more than an hour is to make me ride more relaxed.

We all respond to noise in a similar way. We're used to noise being something that alerts or startles us, and loud noise does just that. Cutting down the incoming noise relaxes your mind and body, which makes you a better rider. I've found that it doesn't hurt my ability to hear cars, either, even with a helmet.

Note: Earplugs are not legal in some states.

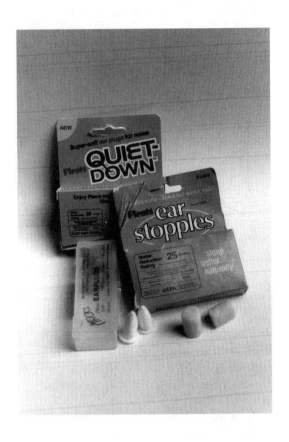

The Gut Remains

"Oh, what a disgusting article," said my friend and occasional proofreader when she saw the first draft of this piece, written right after Christmas.

It may be disgusting, but, hey—in the holiday season we eat, drink, and be merry, for tomorrow we diet. And until that time, we're all at risk for stomach problems. In fact, we all overindulge occasionally—not just around the holidaze.

Indigestion

One big risk we have at such times of year (besides all the kids on the new bikes they got for Christmas) is indigestion. You might say, "what's a chapter on indigestion doing in a book on motorcycle medicine?" Good question!

Puking

Indigestion isn't new. In ancient Rome, heavy-duty pigging-out was the rule of the day. It wasn't unusual to have banquets go on for hours, and you couldn't just refuse to eat, either. So what did the Romans do? They used the vomitorium, which was exactly what it sounds like, and went back to eat more and more.

I'm not recommending we all go off in the bathroom and puke after the first few courses. For one thing, it's in poor taste. Ever see Monty Python's *The Meaning of Life?* You know what I mean.

There's a condition called "bulimia" characterized by people vomiting on purpose to keep down their weight. Pretty wretched, huh? But, if you find yourself stuffed with God knows what, diluted with booze, and are about to worship at the porcelain altar— hey, go for it. You'll feel better afterward.

Antacids

If you're a little queasy, take some antacid. My favorite is Lemon Swiss Cream flavored Maalox, but I haven't seen that one around for a while. For occasional use, any brand will do. Tums will do fine. So will Alka-Seltzer.

The Runs

Another G.I. (gastro-intestinal) complaint is diarrhea, popularly called "the runs," "the trots," or, if related to travel south of the border, "the Montezuma two-step." In that case, the runs are due to a couple of species of bacteria fighting it out in your gut. This often happens soon after going to a new area or a foreign country. It can be prevented with Pepto-Bismol a few times a day. This would be good stuff to take if you're planning on a long ride out in the boonies of, say, Mexico. Either that or pull a Porta Potti on a trailer (Winnebago-type bike makers take note: another option could be the Porta Potti for bikes! It could fit under the driver's saddle, or maybe in a saddle bag!).

There are a few reasons for diarrhea. One is that there's something in your gut that's irritating it. Another is that there's an infection in your gut that your body's trying to get rid of. In either case, it doesn't make much sense to take something that'll keep whatever the problem is around longer. Best plan is to "sit it out," so to speak.

Kaopectate Problems

The most commonly recommended stuff for the runs is Kaopectate, a mixture of kaolin and pectin, found respectively beneath banana and apple skins. They're supposed to thicken up your b.m. and fix the problem. It's a nice theory but it doesn't work well. You'd have to drink so much of the stuff to make it effective that it's just not worthwhile.

Lomotil Problems

Another often prescribed medicine for the "two-step" is Lomotil. This is a mixture of diphenoxylate (a narcotic) and atropine (which makes it hard to get high with the narcotic). Narcotics slow down your bowels—just ask any narcotic user. In fact, they work too well. If you take narcotics (including Lomotil) too much, you end up with a fecal impaction. Getting a fecal impaction out is a real pain in the—well, it's uncomfortable. I think you should only take Lomotil if you absolutely CAN'T have diarrhea for a few hours. After all, if something's in your gut that's either an irritation or an infection, why keep it around? Get the sh*t out'a there! Imodium is also very good at stopping diarrhea, like Lomotil, but doesn't need a prescription.

Barfing

Having to barf (that's a technical term, folks) all the time is almost as bad as having the runs. Though there are medicines that stop vomiting, they'll also make you real sleepy. NOT recommended for riding, or driving, for that matter.

Dehydration

If you have been vomiting, don't let yourself get dehydrated! When your body gets dried out (dehydrated) it makes you feel more nauseated and more likely to throw up again. A vicious circle, in other words. One way to prevent dehydration is to get fluids into the body a little at a time.

Remember—if your stomach is twitchy, don't try putting a whole glass of water or Gatorade or whatever in it at once. It'll just clench up and say "back to you, Frank," and you'll be back where you started.

The way to get fluids down into a twitchy stomach is to take it slow. I recommend parents use a teaspoon to give toddlers one teaspoon at a time, about once a minute. This'll get enough fluids into the body to prevent getting dried out. Works on adults, too.

Foods

Avoid dairy products on an upset stomach; they hurt more than they help. Avoid spicy, rich, and greasy food, too. The best foods to baby your tummy (or a baby's tummy, for that matter) are things like bananas, rice, applesauce, and dry toast. (The acronym for remembering this stuff is B-R-A-T.) Wait 'til it's quieted down for at least a day before going back to a diet that's hard on the digestive tract.

If you've had a lot of diarrhea and/or vomiting and are getting dried out, you have to drink stuff in addition to water. Gatorade is good, since it has electrolytes in it. Don't give straight Gatorade to babies, though—it might be too concentrated for them to handle. Ask their pediatrician. Fruit juices are OK, too.

In the end, though, don't get upset about a bout of stomach flu or the Montezuma two-step. Be philosophical. In fact, consider taking to heart the motto

on the bumper sticker I have over my computer:
SHIT HAPPENS!

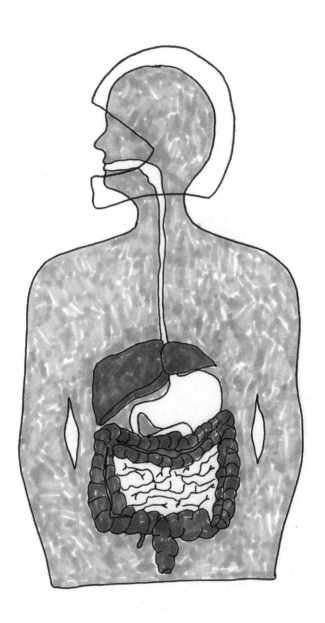

Duh Thrill of Victory, Duh Agony of Duh Feet

Feet. What do ya need to know about 'em? Well, feet have toes which are easy to break. Folks often ask if they need X rays on their injured toe after kicking something. If the bad toe's lined up with the other toes, and the joints don't seem to hurt when they're bent (gently), and it's not the big toe, I tell 'em that even if it is broken, most likely they'd just get it taped. The main reasons for getting an X ray would be for legal reasons, if you need to document an injury, or if you need to know how long it'll keep hurting. If it's broken, it'll hurt for a couple of weeks. If bruised, it'll probably just hurt for a few days. Of course, if it's badly broken, it'll probably need X rays. If you're in doubt as to whether it's BADLY broken or not, see your health care delivery person.

Broken Toes

Once you've determined that your toe is injured—but that it still looks like a toe and that the joints work—what to do? "Buddy-tape" the li'l sucker. This limits its motion, which makes it feel better. To buddy-tape a toe, first put something absorbent between it and the next toe so the skin doesn't get sweaty and break down. Gauze, cotton, or even a few layers of paper towel or paper napkin work. Tape the toe to the one inside of it, but not to the big toe; that is, tape an injured #2 toe to your #3 toe, a bad #3 to #2, #4 to #3, and #5 to #4. To tape, take a narrow strip of tape (half-inch adhesive works best) and tape as close to the foot as you can, in the middle, and near the end of the toe. Not too tight: it should just keep the toe from moving much.

Buddy-Taping

After injury, ALWAYS elevate the injured part. It's especially important for toes, since they can

Swelling

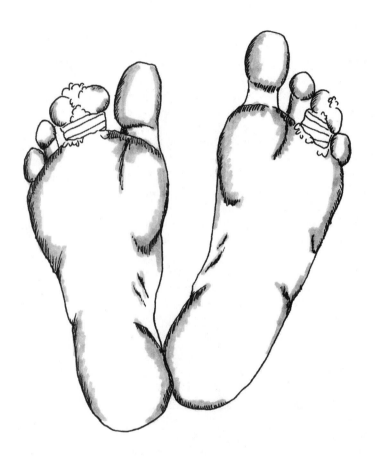

swell and hurt more if not kept up. Icing it is a REAL good idea, too. Ice will relieve pain and prevent swelling. Ice and elevation can change an injury from one that could keep you off your feet for a few days to one that you can walk on in the morning.

Toes also get heavy things dropped on 'em. So, wear boots. After injury, if the toe hurts to move, treat as above. If the nail is dark blue in color, there's probably blood under the nail—a "sub-ungual hematoma" in med-speak. Fresh sub-ungual hematomas throb every time your heart beats and hurt to use. To relieve them, see your health care provider A.S.A.P. If that's not an option, just get the blood out without getting germs in. Here's how: first clean the nail with alcohol or soap and water. Take a 2-inch section of paper clip or similar sized wire and stick it in a cork. Then heat the wire tip RED HOT and press it into the middle of the blue part of your nail (make sure the alcohol is dry before you try this—otherwise you may end up with roast toes). You'll feel a temporary resistance; you'll hear the nail sizzle; and then the nail will "give" as the hot wire melts through. The hotter it is, the faster it'll do this. When the tip goes through the nail, pull back quickly. A couple of drops of blood will come through the hole, and the throbbing will stop! You'll feel 90% better in seconds. Cover the hole in your nail with some antibiotic ointment or, better, zinc oxide, and then put a loose Band-Aid on it. Keep it clean and avoid swimming for a few days. Watch for infection, too.

Blue Toenail

And then there's athlete's foot. It's your body's reaction to a fungus that eats the dead skin between your toes. IMPORTANT NOTE: ATHLETE'S FOOT DOESN'T HURT! IF IT DOES, IT'S INFECTED WITH BACTERIA AND SHOULD BE TAKEN CARE OF WITHOUT DELAY! Treatment for INFECTED athlete's foot includes antibiotics, which you'd have to get from your doc. Itchy (non-infected) athlete's foot should be treated with anti-fungals, such as miconazole, available over the counter as Micatin. Other over-the-counter remedies don't work as well, in my experience. To prevent recur-

Athlete's Foot

rences, use athlete's foot meds at least four or five days after you're better.

It's good to keep your foot from coming in contact with shower floors other than your own. When traveling or in the gym, wearing flip-flops in the shower will prevent most athlete's foot infections.

Of Phlegm and Men

When flu season comes around, people hack and cough everywhere you go. You end up with friends or co-workers who are down with "the bug." So what do YOU do?

Since there's no cure for most of these bugs, it's important to keep from catching 'em. Avoid inhaling other people's sneezes. Don't kiss unhealthy folks. Most important, wash your hands a lot. That's because most people catch "the bug" by picking up germs with their hands, and then touching a mucous membrane like their mouth, nose or eyes.

The kind of "bug" that seems to cause the most trouble is the one that starts with a sore throat and/or a cold, followed by a cough that settles into your chest. It's not technically a "flu," which is short for influenza.

Influenza is a disease caused by one of a certain group of viruses called, logically enough, influenza viruses. Influenza can be treated with certain drugs that will often make it less severe or totally prevent you from getting it. However, most "flu" is NOT influenza. There aren't any drugs to kill the non-influenza "flu."

Smokers seem to be having more trouble than non-smokers, which is only to be expected, considering that they're functioning without a lot of the natural cleaning capabilities of the lungs.

By the way, here's a good statistic: This year, premature deaths from smoking will be greater than those from AIDS, heroin, cocaine, alcohol, traffic accidents, fires, murders, and suicides—combined! In other words, if you quit smoking, you cut your risk of

Preventing Colds

Flu

Smoking

59

death just as much as if you had a magic charm that protected you from all those other causes . . .

Avoid Cold Remedies

What can you do when you've definitely got "it"? Go kiss somebody you hate. (Joking, folks—I'm JUST JOKING!) The first thing is to AVOID THE USE OF COUGH AND COLD REMEDIES! Most of 'em have strong drying agents in 'em—you know, the ingredients that change nice runny snot to hard boogers? (That's a technical term.) They make your nose drip less, but dry it out. They also dry out your lungs. You end up with dried plugs of phlegm in your chest.

Bronchitis

Imagine your chest full of dry boogers, tickling and irritating your bronchial tubes, making you cough up phlegm all the time, and blocking off small sections of your lungs, causing them to get super infected with bacteria. This is called bronchitis. Bronchitis is common after having the "bug," and now you know why.

Cleaning Your Lungs

OK—you've stopped the cold remedies, but you've got a chest full of dried phlegm. How do you get it out? The key word here is "dry." Notice how you cough after a steamy shower? That's because the vapor gets down in your lungs, moistens the dried phlegm, and loosens it up. It then starts to slide in the bronchial tubes, tickling a new area, making you cough. Unfortunately, it usually slides down-the-tubes—and you want it to go up and out. How do you get the stuff up?

Easy. Change up for down. That is, steam up your lungs (a closed bathroom full of steam for five or ten minutes works fine) and then get the stuff out by gravity.

Lie face down on a bed or couch with your head, shoulders, and back hanging downward over the edge, and have somebody pound your back with cupped hands while you breathe as deeply as you can. This will loosen the stuff in your chest enough to let some of it be coughed up and out, which is where you want it. The pounding should last about five to ten minutes, and you should make sure your sides get pounded as well as your back. Have a cup nearby for the phlegm you'll be hacking up.

After getting the phlegm up, check its color. Clear, white, or pale phlegm means that the infection is still just viral, and probably doesn't need antibiotics. If it's dark yellow, green, or brown, or if you're having lots of fevers, chills, chest pains, or have other health problems, antibiotics should be considered.

One very important thing with chest colds and bronchitis: get plenty of fluids. Lack of fluids is a major contributing factor in getting sick in the first place. If you're low on fluids, your phlegm will be that much thicker and harder to get up. You should drink enough extra fluids that when you pee, it comes out just about clear. (Remember that B-vitamins can turn your urine more yellow than usual.) Avoid alcohol as a primary fluid source. It tends to dry you out. Though coffee and tea also tend to dehydrate, they can decrease wheezing in folks with a tendency toward asthma. A humidifier in your bedroom is very helpful, too.

Things to watch for: high fevers not responsive to aspirin or Tylenol, shortness of breath, coughing caused by deep breathing, or painful breathing. If you get any of those symptoms, get in touch with your health care delivery person. Actually, "health care delivery" isn't the right term anymore. How often do you get health care delivered to you? Not very often. YOU have to go get it.

Fluids

Motoholics Anonymous

There are a lot of excellent programs in existence to help folks who have problems with alcohol, with drugs, with being a workaholic—in fact, there's almost every kind of a "somethingorothers anonymous" out there except for one: motoholics anonymous.

Motoholism

I discovered the need for this organization when I got the opportunity to test ride the new BMW K-1 motorcycle. To be honest, as an old BMW twin rider, I never had much use for the K bikes. (K bikes are BMW's new, water-cooled, three and four inline cylinder models.) My initial riding impressions of them were that they were fast, smooth, stable, and boring. They didn't have the "character" that the old twins have. Then I got to ride the K-1.

The first day I rode it, I didn't think much of it. The feet were too high. The riding position wasn't what I was used to. True, it went very quickly and stopped faster than humanly possible with the ABS, and handled more like an Interceptor 500 than a BMW, but still . . . I wasn't sold.

The Process of Addiction

After the second day I rode it, I was more pleased. The footpegs had apparently magically lowered themselves to a more comfortable position, and the riding position seemed better. Plus, the bike got an incredible amount of attention on the street. People stopped and talked about it whenever I parked. Drivers were saying, "What kinda bike is that?" at stop lights. I enjoyed the attention. But still, 13 grand for a bike is a lot.

Getting Hooked

The third day did the trick. I was riding along Haight Street and two women on bikes did U-turns

63

to ask me about it. Whew! Being single and relatively unattached, this facet of K-1 ownership was quite appealing. No women ever made U-turns when I was on the R-0 (my current tricked-out twin).

I even thought about what Chairman Mal (Malcolm Forbes) said not long before he died: "I don't waste time. If there's something that turns me on, I do it now. This life isn't a dry run."

Frantic Indecision

So, I decided to buy the K-1. So what if I'd have to live on beans and rice for the year or three it would take me to pay it off. As long as you ride a bike, eating beans isn't too bad. Cars with closed windows cause the problems. Then, after realizing I couldn't put saddlebags on it, and that my knees probably wouldn't last too long while riding with 'em that close to my armpits, I decided not to buy it. Then, after thinking about the ABS and how nice it acted when I deliberately tried to lock the front brake going over a wet steel plate, I decided to get it. Then, after considering what it would do to my insurance premiums, I decided not to get it. Then, after feeling how smooth and strong and broad the powerband was, I decided to get it.

Salvation

In short, I've been going crazy with this bike. The sensible part of me says: "13 grand for a bike? The R-0 is better in city traffic anyhow. Get real!!" The romantic part of me says "K-1 . . . K-1 . . . K-1 . . ." What I figure I need is a group of some sort where I can go and say, "My name is flash. I'm no longer in control of my life . . . " and talk to other folks who get crazy around motorcycles. I need somebody I can call up at ten at night and say, "Quick! Tell me why I shouldn't buy this bike!" In short, I need motoholics anonymous.

Anybody wanna start a chapter? We could meet, say, Sunday mornings up in Marin county where the Sunday morning ride starts . . .

Hemorrhoids are a "fundamental" problem in today's society. In fact, it's said that to be a successful political leader, one needs "glasses for the look of intelligence, white hair for the look of sincerity, and hemorrhoids for the look of concern."

Hemorrhoids are no laughing matter. Some historians believe that Napoleon lost the Battle of Waterloo because his hemorrhoids kept him from sleeping the night before. If you've got hemorrhoids now or have had them in the past, I'm sure you can sympathize.

Motorcyclists are particularly at risk for hemorrhoids, especially those of us who ride for quite a while without stretching or taking a break. Take my word for it: your Gold Wing is good for more miles non-stop than you are!

What are hemorrhoids? They're those little bulges felt around the anus (anus is medical for asshole, but I'm not allowed to write that word), often more prominent after a bowel movement. Functionally, they're veins, similar to varicose veins. When you bear down and increase the pressure in your chest, it increases the pressure in the hemorrhoidal veins and makes them bulge. This particular factor often happens during pregnancy, when the swollen womb pushes on the blood vessels returning to the heart; when you're coughing a lot, and each cough sends a wave of pressure throughout your venous system; when you spend too much time on the toilet causing the hemorrhoidal veins to bulge; and most commonly, when your bowel movements are too hard, and you have to push down extra hard for extra long.

The best thing to do when any of the above occur is to soften your stool. Softer stool needs less pushing—consequently, there's less bulging and less possibility of . . . THROMBOSED HEMORRHOIDS!

Thrombosed hemorrhoids are just hemorrhoids with a clot inside them, but at that time they really become a pain in the . . . well, let's just say that they create a sensation not unlike having a hot brick in your butt. When small and uncomplicated (that is, when smaller than a marble), this sensation typically lasts two to three days. You can count on "the look of concern" being present almost continually during this time. The sensation will gradually fade, usually disappearing completely within a week after the beginning of the episode.

Treatment

Treatment for thrombosed hemorrhoids during the episode is a combination of stool softeners (a psyllium seed husk preparation, such as Perdiem or Metamucil, taken one to three times daily), pain meds (an over-the-counter med such as ibuprofen provides pain relief without constipation), and most importantly, sitz baths. Many patients ask, "How do I do a sitz bath?" Simple! You put a few inches of hot water into the bath tub, and you sitz in the bath. It really helps, and the more often, the better. In fact, if you're taking enough sitz baths, your toes will start to look like prunes.

Another treatment for acutely thrombosed hemorrhoids is numbing up the skin over the culprit with Xylocaine, cutting off the top, and then lifting out the clot that's causing the problem. Some people who have had them treated both ways prefer the surgery; others prefer the conservative treatment described above. If it's as big as the last joint of your thumb, have it cut.

Prevention

The best way to prevent (and to treat) hemorrhoids is by eating enough roughage to give you large, soft stools. This avoids straining while having a bowel movement, which causes hemorrhoids. You get roughage from green leafy vegetables like lettuce; from commercial stool softeners like

Metamucil or Perdiem; and from bran, which you can find in a lot of breakfast cereals. You can judge if you're getting enough roughage by (sorry) the end result.

The bottom line (sorry again) is this: hemorrhoids are a common problem in today's society. Exercise, a good diet, healthy bowel habits, and getting those magazines out of the bathroom should go a long way in preventing them. Sitz baths, stool softeners, and occasionally surgery are the cure. Those of us who've had them agree: they can be a real pain in the . . . um, er . . . well, let's put it this way—you should always try to PREVENT hemorrhoids, since you only have one . . . um, er . . . *.

A*******k

* This symbol is called an asterisk. Read the last sentence above, pronouncing it out loud. Now hit your forehead and say "duh!!"

How Dry I Am??

Some folks put their bikes away for the wet season, but not me. Riding in the rain's not bad, if you pay attention to a few details.

Rain

First thing to keep in mind is you won't have much traction in the wet. Rain grooves or no rain grooves, when the first heavy rain floats all that oil out of the cracks in the street, it'll be slicker than snail slime on Teflon, as one good friend used to say. Be extra careful on painted letters like "EXIT" or "STOP." Avoid braking, accelerating, or turning on them.

Slick

Wet paint can be lethal when you're braking to slow down and get off the freeway. Suddenly, both wheels are sliding; and then you are, too. The way to prevent this is to brake *slowly* and gradually.

Braking

Wet disc brakes vary in their ability to stop a bike. I've been riding downhill in the mountains in the rain only to find my front twin discs are almost useless. Luckily, the BMWs I usually ride have a rear drum brake, which works when wet. You really should get into the habit of checking braking ability once things get damp.

It's also possible to heat up your brakes by riding with them slightly on for ten or fifteen seconds at a time. The heat will dry them off. Be careful not to overheat them.

Visibility is another rain-related problem. You can't see traffic, and it can't see you. It's sometimes particularly bad if you drive a bike with a tall windshield. For safety's sake, make sure you can see over the top. My Parabellum shield is designed to deflect air over my face, leaving a clear area to see through.

Visibility

Having a helmet face shield that locks open at various stages is good, since it will allow you to have nothing but air in front of your eyes, weather permitting. The BMW System 2 does that well.

Face Shields

Sometimes, when it's raining hard, you're going to need to keep the face shield closed. To clean it, you can wear gloves with a soft patch on the back, like some Thurlow's, that can be used for wiping the shield clear. This works fairly well. The best trick I've found, though, is the mini "visor-wiper" made by Metzeler. It's a rubber squeegee that fits over one finger, that works just like a wiper blade.

Bright Clothing

It's not good enough just to see the other drivers, though: you need to be seen yourself. When it's really nasty out, I'll wear a yellow foul-weather slicker over my leathers, both to stay dryer and to be seen. I'd also wear a Conspicuity "visibility vest" if I were going to be riding at night in the rain. It's made of mesh with several VERY reflective stripes on it. I also make it a point of checking my tail light AND my brake light before riding in miserable conditions.

Hypothermia

A big danger in wet riding is one of the most subtle: hypothermia. I'll talk more about that in the next chapter.

Too Cool is Not Too Cool

Most of us have been cold at one time or another. It's one thing to feel a little chilly—it's quite another to be hypothermic to the point where your thinking and reflexes are slowed enough to be dangerous if you're on a bike.

Hypothermia just means "low temperature" in Latin. We usually run at 98.6 degrees—but if we drop a couple of degrees below that, we shiver. When we shiver, our muscles generate heat, which warms the body. We get into trouble when we're losing heat faster than we can make it.

My first personal experience with hypothermia was in the late 1970s, riding from Yosemite to Gilroy in the rain. I'd loaned a friend my rain suit to use on our rafting trip—and he'd managed to rip the jacket wide open. I was wearing long underwear, a T-shirt, a couple of wool shirts, my leather jacket, and the torn rain jacket over that. I also had on blue jeans and rain pants. The temperature was in the fifties.

The rain leaked through the torn jacket pretty quickly. Then the leather jacket got soaked; so did the rest of my clothes from the waist up. I started shivering. I stopped for coffee, which helped some, but continued despite my shivers. Pretty soon I was shivering hard enough to have trouble holding on to the handlebars.

I wasn't really thinking straight by this time. I just kept thinking that I had to get to the party in Gilroy; the thought that it would be safer to stop and get warmer never crossed my mind. That's a big danger with hypothermia—your judgment can be

Being Cold

Being Really Cold

My Hypothermic Story

71

affected without you knowing it. Riding while hypothermic can be as bad as riding drunk.

Getting Warm

Luckily, I arrived in one piece. My temperature didn't even register on the thermometer, which went down to 94. I was shivering so hard I couldn't hold the coffee my friend Skip gave me. I took off all my wet stuff and climbed into a hot bathtub with some brandy in my coffee. After a while I put on dry clothes from my tank bag and borrowed two down jackets from people at the party. I started feeling better after another couple of hours of shivering.

Getting Buzzed

The shot of brandy in my coffee was OK only because I was in a warm place and not riding again that night. Alcohol opens up the circulation to your extremities, so it's OK to drink a little once you're out of the cold, but it's bad if you're still in a position to lose heat.

Getting Snuggly

Another way to get your body temperature up is to snuggle up under the covers with a warm person of the appropriate gender.

In fact, if you want to try this, go ahead and tell the person, "It's doctor's orders! Honest!!"

Let me know if it works.

Hats

There's an old saying, "If your feet are cold, put on a hat." This makes good sense. When your feet get cold, it's an early sign that you're low on body heat. Our bodies can only make heat so fast—and when we start running low, we need to stop losing it. Blood flow to our arms and legs gets turned down to save heat.

Windchill Factor

Your head is a big source of heat loss. Covering it helps a lot, especially if there's any wind. The higher the wind, the more the windchill factor. Windchill factor is just a way of estimating how much heat will be carried away by the wind. You blow on something hot to cool it—that works on your body, too. That's why riding in 55-degree weather can chill us badly, even though standing around in the same clothes might be comfortable.

Clothes

Layering

To stay warm in the cold, you have to keep wind off your skin. That's why leather is so great—not only is it abrasion resistant, it's almost completely wind-proof. Wearing a bunch of layers under that helps, too, by keeping warm air next to your skin. Long underwear can change a nasty cold ride to a pleasant one. Besides, if you lose your jeans, you can just pretend you're being fashionable and walk around in your long johns . . .

Another useful item that prevents heat loss is a silk long-sleeved undershirt. I bought one for $18.50 mail order from L.L. Bean. It provides an amazing amount of warmth for its weight and size. In fact, I now keep one on the bike for those times I get caught away from home and it gets chillier than expected. Polypropylene is even better.

Silk Undershirt

I've also successfully used deerskin gloves made by Thurlow. They come both lined and unlined, and you can buy thin silk undergloves that help in real cold. Back in Boston, I used to use "Hippo Hands," which were padded nylon handlebar covers that strapped onto the bike itself. They were great. Naturally, you'll want to wear a T-shirt, a wool shirt, and maybe a sweater if it's on the cold side.

Gloves, Etc.

Of course, if you drive a Winnebago-style bike, complete with digital compass, cigarette lighter, stereo, and beer can holder, you won't have much problem with the cold. The fairing will take care of that. Still, for those cold days, an electric vest will probably keep you nice and toasty. (I personally like the ones by Saingear: 415 591-2373.) And, hey—why not go the whole nine yards, and get electric gloves, chaps and socks, too? If your bike's set up for it— well, more power to you . . .

Winnebago Toasters

"Sh*t, That Was Close!!!"

You just narrowly avoided being obliterated by a van that came around a blind corner halfway into your lane. You can feel your heart pounding; your muscles might be shaking a bit; and you're hoping you don't need clean underwear just yet (like Bill Cosby says: "First you say it; then you do it.").

Close Call

What you're experiencing is the effect of epinephrine on your body. Often called the "fight or flight" reaction, this is simply the result of the epinephrine (or adrenaline) that your adrenal glands pump into your system when maximum effort is required. Think of it as downshifting two gears and popping the clutch.

Adrenaline

We all know what gives us the adrenaline "rush." Typically, it's a situation that promotes fear or anger—or both. We recognize it by the pounding of our hearts, heavy breathing, and often a heightened clarity of thought and vision. It's just the body getting ready to do something that might be needed for survival.

A lot of people like the feeling. That might be why they ride fast—and sometimes dangerously. Some people like the feeling so much that they become "adrenaline junkies," doing everything in a way that builds pressure, letting 'em savor the pressure that comes from having to do something at the last minute, sweating under pressure.

Adrenaline Junkies

Here's what happens to your body when it gets the jolt of adrenaline: first, your heart rate speeds up. This is to provide you with extra blood flow to supply your muscles in case you have to "fight or

What Happens

flee." Your breathing gets faster for the same reason. In extreme cases, your bowel empties itself (that's a pound or two less stuff to carry around—and if you're being chased by a saber-toothed tiger, that pound might make a difference) and your thinking gets clearer.

Drug Effects & Adrenaline Effects

This sounds a lot like the effect some people get from certain drugs, like speed or coke. They do have some parallel in how they work, as a matter of fact. The difference between stimulants and adrenaline is that some stimulants artificially tweak the part of your brain responsible for saying "hey, this feels good." We all have part of our brains that does that. Usually, though, it gets tweaked when we do something that is good for us, like eating when we're hungry, or drinking when we're thirsty, or peeing when we need to, or sleeping—you get the idea. With stimulants, though, the "feelgood center" gets tweaked to the point that people ignore things like eating, drinking, sleeping, grooming, sex, and even riding their bikes . . . (if you can imagine that).

Type A Adrenaline Junkie

I was a classic Type A personality, and Type As are often adrenaline junkies (see previous chapter). Type As have two main characteristics: "free-floating hostility" and a sense of time urgency called "hurry sickness." We "flare up" and become angry, irritated, annoyed and/or impatient for trivial reasons, releasing a lot of catecholamines (like adrenaline) into our systems, causing our hearts to beat harder and pump faster and producing those feelings of alertness, strength, and power—which are much like the feelings produced by cocaine or speed.

Type A Personality

Here's how being an "adrenaline freak" can affect your personality, especially if you didn't get enough unconditional love as a child and have some feelings of doubt about yourself, deep down:

Adrenaline Freak

> *Type A behavior is above all a continuous struggle, an unremitting attempt to accomplish or achieve more and more things or participate in more and more events in less and less time, frequently in the face of opposition, real or imagined, from other persons. The Type A personality is dominated by covert insecurity of status or hyperaggressiveness, or both.*
>
> *It is one or both of these two basic components that generally causes the struggle to begin. The struggle itself sooner or later fosters the emergence of a third personality ingredient, that sense of time urgency we have designated hurry sickness. As the struggle continues, the hyperaggressiveness (and also*

Type A Dynamics

perhaps the status insecurity) usually shows itself in the easily aroused anger we term free-floating hostility. Finally, if the struggle becomes severe enough and persists long enough, it may lead to a fifth component, a tendency toward self-destruction.

As the above description implies, Type A behavior erupts most frequently in a person already aggressive and unsure about his status when he encounters situations that he construes as either status-threatening or irritating and anger-provoking. It is only then that the struggle ensues, bringing in its wake a sense of time urgency or free-floating hostility, and, after the passage of many years, the tendency to self-destruct.

(From Treating Type A Behavior and Your Heart, by Meyer Friedman, M.D., and Diane Ulmer, R.N., M.S.)

Addiction

Speed and coke are extremely psychologically addictive. This implies that adrenaline is psychologically addictive, too. I've had lots of experience with substance abuse, both with patients (at the Haight Ashbury Free Medical Clinic) and elsewhere, so I decided to treat myself like an adrenaline junkie.

Treatment

I imagined I had a little "Type A adrenaline junkie/demon" sitting on my shoulder looking for excuses to get mad or impatient (any of the Type A behaviors) so he could get my body to make more adrenaline, which is the Type A adrenaline junkie/demon's drug of choice. Realizing that, it suddenly made sense why I'd get pissed off for no good reason—my demon just wanted its hit of adrenaline! I visualized the demon like an evil Jiminy Cricket sitting on Mickey Mouse's shoulder.

I decided to experiment. I would treat the adrenaline junkie/demon like I would a substance abuse patient, and not let him bullshit his way into doing any adrenaline needlessly. Adrenaline is useful at times—but we just don't often have to flee saber-toothed tigers in downtown San Francisco.

I found that "externalizing" and thinking of the adrenaline junkie/ demon as an opponent appealed to my competitive instincts. Every time I successfully denied the adrenaline junkie/demon its hit of "natural dope," I scored a point, and gave myself an appropriate psychic pat on the back—"way to go"!! I'd even reward myself with a Life Saver or small piece of candy.

I soon found I was routinely preventing the adrenaline junkie/demon from scoring at all. It became unable to get even a little bit of the adrenaline power/rush. Interestingly, it became easier and easier to control it over a period of just a few days. It really felt good to be in control of myself, not allowing some bozo in a car or clerk in a post office jerk me around by my own autonomic nervous system. I could generate a berserker rage if I needed one—but who needs it? I don't feel like dropping dead just yet. And the nicest feeling is defeating that adrenaline junkie/demon who's almost killed me by giving me two coronaries, job friction, and some messed-up relationships in the past.

Since writing the above, I had to have an emergency balloon angioplasty done on myself because of a sudden increase in angina, which often is a warning that you're about to have a heart attack. My thanks to Dr. Ralph Boucher at the San Francisco Heart Institute and all the staff at Seton Medical Center for a most professional job characterized by extreme competence, consideration and caring . . . and thanks to Dr. Meyer Friedman and Diane Ulmer for providing me with the tools to defeat the adrenaline junkie / demon and start enjoying life a lot more.

Gaining Control

Getting old isn't bad, when you consider the alternative. At least, that's what I used to think when I was younger. Much younger. Now that I'm starting to get a little gray and tattered around the edges, I'm beginning to wonder a little. One question that's crossed my mind has been, "Am I getting too old to ride, now that I'm past 40?" I don't think so. The human body ages fairly predictably. Memory loss, for example, is the second notable sign of aging. What's the first? Hmmmm ... Well, I don't recall. Memory loss can be insidious, but I THINK my memory used to be a lot better. I think. Maybe ... More seriously, the first thing to go in most people is their degree of physical conditioning, unless they work real hard at keeping it up. We probably can't run as far, stay up as long, or bounce back from an injury as quickly as we could when we were in our twenties.

This has some direct implications when it comes to riding motorcycles. For example, if you have a particularly stressful get-off and end up with some road rash and a lot of bruises, you'll be back on your feet a lot faster if you're in your twenties than if you're on the high side of 40, particularly if you haven't been working at staying in shape.

Also, as you get older your bones start to lose calcium. This is a direct result of lack of use: weight bearing exercise will cause bones to stay strong. Women in particular should watch for osteoporosis (which can be thought of as "thinning" of the bones) and need to take supplemental calcium and do regular exercise after menopause. Hormone therapy can help women, too.

Aging

Memory Loss

Physical Condition

Accidents

Bones

Most all older bones are just more brittle than young bones. A fall that just gives a young person an impressive black and blue mark often results in a hip fracture in someone with osteoporosis.

Riding Style

Riding style makes a difference, too. I'd be more concerned about the health of a 68 year-old who was going canyon racing on an FZR than the same person taking a Gold Wing across the country. A bad fall (which would probably be more likely from the racer than the tourer) would do more harm in an older person.

Driving habits are also part of the equation. Folks who drive like squids, zipping in and out of traffic, sooner or later will have the odds catch up to them.

The motorcycle itself makes a BIG impact on the potential for an accident. When I was test riding a big Harley cruiser for CityBike, I felt safe, comfortable, and relaxed while on the bike. I could even lean over and tuck my pants in my boots without feeling as if I were taking my life into my hands. I'd never do that on my BMW. I'm not surprised Malcolm Forbes rode a Harley—in fact, I realized that when I grow up a little more and lose my overly aggressive riding tendencies, I'd be perfectly happy on one.

Keep Riding!

So should older folks keep riding? Absolutely! The benefits from getting out of the house, doing things, traveling, fresh air, and so on vastly outweigh the risks involved, especially if the person who's going to be going riding has a few decades of experience under his or her belt. I know I plan to ride until I'm no longer able to do so. And I'll know when I start having accidents, getting tickets, dropping the bike, or otherwise getting messages from the universe that it's time to stop.

"What are the other risk factors I have for a heart attack?" Jeff asked. "I know my cholesterol is high—about 230—and I really messed up with my diet over the last few months."

"The main risk factors for heart disease are a family history of heart disease, high blood pressure, high cholesterol, smoking and sedentary life style. You've got five for five. What are you doing to change them?"

"I can't. It's so hard getting motivated that when I thought about trying, I got so upset I fell off the wagon and started drinking again, and when I started drinking I started smoking again. I tried to quit smoking, and gained 10 pounds. Now what?"

"Have you ever tried that technique I told you about last time: writing a letter to yourself?"

"No, I haven't. How could that help?"

"Well, think about it. Who's got the most to benefit from your staying healthy?"

"Me."

"Right. And who's got the most to lose if you have a heart attack?"

"Me."

"Correct-o. Now, who's in the best position to influence your behavior? Who knows you best?"

"Me."

"Correct again. Who could do the best job at blackmailing you into doing something, like giving up booze or going on a diet?"

"Me."

Heart Disease

How to
Change a
Deadly
Lifestyle

"Amazingly right. Now, here's an interesting way to influence your own behavior. Just sit right down and write yourself a letter . . . (boop, boop, boop)."

"Huh?"

How to Write a Letter to Yourself

"Never mind. Just write a really strong, personal letter to yourself. Explain that you're the person who cares about what happens to you the most (with good cause) and why you need to make some changes. You can get as personal as you want to in this letter, because nobody but you will ever see it. Use whatever emotional jujitsu you want to. It'll stay private. Then, go ahead and mail the letter to yourself. By having it go out into the universe and returning a day or six later (you know the post office), it acquires some special magic effects. When you open it and read it, it'll make a much bigger impression on you than you can imagine. But, when you write it, you've got to write it from the heart. That's the only way it'll work."

"I understand how I can tell myself about smoking and being overweight, but what can I tell myself about high blood pressure? I don't feel tense. Besides, what harm can a little high blood pressure do?"

High Blood Pressure

"Look, Jeff," I replied. "Hypertension doesn't mean you're 'too tense.' It means your blood pressure is up—and you don't usually feel that at all.

"The problem with high blood pressure is that your heart has to work harder on each stroke. The heart is just a muscle that pumps blood—and if it works harder, it'll get thicker muscles."

"Isn't that good?"

Heart Disease

"No. Think of it like this. When you pump iron, the muscles in your arms get bigger. When your heart exercises by pumping against more pressure, the muscles in its wall get thicker. Since most of the blood supply to the heart comes from the outside surface, the thicker the muscle, the harder it is to get blood all the way through it.

"Now, blood is what carries the oxygen and nutrients that keep your heart alive. If a piece of heart muscle doesn't get an adequate blood supply, you'll get either angina (which you can think of as a charley horse or cramp in your heart muscle, due to relative lack of blood), or an infarct, which is where the piece of heart muscle that's not getting adequate blood actually can die from lack of oxygen and nutrients. This is like a stroke, in a way. It's called a heart attack.

"You should think of high blood pressure as the equivalent of adding a little weight to the end of a barbell that your heart is working out with. Every time it beats, the extra 'weight' makes it a little more muscular. And that's bad."

"Doesn't stress cause high blood pressure?"

Stress

"Well, stress can add to it, and it's definitely worthwhile to reduce stress where and when you can. You might be able to reduce your need for medication by reducing stress, cutting down salt intake and watching your diet. Losing weight and getting some regular aerobic exercise also reduces your cardiac risk, and might help your blood pressure, too."

Reducing Cardiac Risk

"Boy, people always tell me the same thing: lose some weight, stop drinking and smoking as much, reduce stress, eat right, and get some exercise. That's all I ever hear!"

"Of course you keep hearing it," I said. "It's true."

"That's the Breaks"

The clavicle, or collarbone, is one of the most frequently broken bones in the body, especially in folks who ride motorcycles, bicycles, or horses.

Collarbones

The clavicle can break when you fall onto your shoulder. It works as a "rod" that keeps the "ball joint" in your shoulder from getting too close to your chest. Impact on the outside or back of the shoulder causes direct force to be exerted onto the clavicle, which then breaks.

How it Breaks

The clavicle is also easy to break with a direct blow to its middle. When I was learning hand-to-hand combat, this was drilled into us many times. "It only takes eight pounds of pressure to break the collarbone," we were told. It's not a hard bone to break.

If you break a clavicle, you'll know it. It'll hurt, and the collarbone won't be shaped like the other one (assuming it matched). There will be a tender bump in the clavicle. Moving the shoulder will hurt.

Treatment is simple: make it not hurt. I don't mean "drink or dope yourself into a stupor." I mean immobilize the shoulder.

Treatments

A simple way to do this temporarily is to do what's called a "sling and swath." This is just a sling supporting the arm on the injured side and something wrapped around the upper arm and chest to keep it from moving. It'll feel much better when it's not being used: however, if you find yourself in a situation where you MUST use that arm, the sling and swath will be a problem.

A "figure of eight" dressing is another, better way to treat a broken clavicle. Since the clavicle is basically a support to keep the shoulder joint from falling forward, the figure of eight dressing just pulls the shoulder joint back, and takes pressure off the broken bone.

Figure of Eight Dressing

Here's how to make a figure of eight dressing: first, you need a long (maybe four to five yards) strip of cloth, or a three to four inch wide elastic bandage. You then put a pad under each armpit, so the cloth won't rub. A handkerchief or a sock makes an adequate pad. Next, have the victim sit down facing away from you. His shoulders should be as far back as possible: in fact, he should try to make them meet in the middle of the back. Having them this far back pulls the broken ends of the clavicle apart so they won't grind together.

Ugh.

Starting at the middle of the back between the shoulder blades, roll the wrap up over the good shoulder, down, around, and under the good armpit, back up over the middle of the back between the shoulder blades again, up over the bad shoulder, down, around, and through the bad armpit, back up to the middle of the small of the back, and repeat. And repeat. And repeat.

I like to use Kerlix gauze bandages for this. They're one item that should be in serious first aid kits.

Trauma Check

After any injury like this, it's important to do a couple of things. First, make sure the rest of the person is OK. It's not a good idea to patch somebody's broken clavicle and miss a broken neck. Doing a one minute trauma check on folks who fall from bikes, cycles, or horses is a very good idea (see the following chapter on Checking an Accident Victim).

It's possible, but unlikely, for a broken clavicle to puncture a lung or injure a large blood vessel or nerve. If this is the case, there isn't a lot you can do about it in the field. Get the person to medical attention as soon as possible.

Last, and most important, if you're going to be traveling in an area where medical help isn't readily available, be prepared to take care of yourself and your companions. Taking a first aid course is a good beginning. Reading and having a book like *Medicine for Mountaineering and Other Wilderness Activities (4th ed.)*, edited by James A. Wilkerson, M.D. (Seattle, WA: The Mountaineers, 1992) is an excellent idea.

If you're going to be on your own away from civilization a lot, try to take an EMT (emergency medical technician) training course, too. A lot of it is aimed at teaching you the evaluation and initial care of folks in MVAs (motor vehicle accidents). It could come in real handy someday.

It could even save a life.

Checking an Accident Victim

. . . So you look in your rear view mirror and she's down. "Uh-oh," you mutter to yourself as you hang a U-turn and head back. When you get off your bike, she's sitting in the road next to her new bike. "What happened?" you ask. "I just lost it in the turn," she replies, "and I think I broke my wrist. And my knee hurts like hell. Do you think we need to call an ambulance?" "Well . . . "

One Minute
Trauma Check

Now's the time it pays to do a one minute trauma check. Here's what you do:

First, you DON'T MOVE HER UNTIL SHE'S CHECKED!!! Assuming, of course, she's not lying in a burning vehicle or about to be done in by another hazard. The risk in moving her is that you might make an injury worse—pull dirt into an open wound, for example, or have a closed fracture become open by the bone poking through the skin, or (and this is the real killer) have her broken neck suddenly paralyze her. This happens. You can break the bones and even dislocate them in the neck without injuring the spinal cord. Movement can shear through it like a brick hitting a piece of overcooked asparagus.

Don't Move
the Victim!!

The first thing to do is ask her "What happened?" Even if you saw the accident, this is important. It will tell you not only what may have happened, but also give you a good idea of her overall function. An answer of "Well, I was comin' around this corner and was looking back over my shoulder at the marquee at the movie theater," tells you her brain (the technical term for brain is "squash"), throat, lungs and chest are working OK. On the other hand, if she just

Ask What
Happened

says "Arrrrrrgh . . . ," start to worry. If she answers by saying, "I was just (gasp) coming around (gasp) the corner (gasp) and I was looking (gasp) . . . ," and so on, there's obviously something going on. Bad shortness of breath right after a bad accident is a bad sign.

Ask About the Neck

Next, ask about her neck. I've seen people who've WALKED into the E.R. a few days after breaking their necks. Plus, broken necks tend to get worse, not better, without proper care. Tell her to lie perfectly still and ask if there is any pain at all in her neck. If she says yes, you have to assume it is broken until proven otherwise. If she says no, then go ahead with the rest of the neck exam.

Check the Neck

Without moving her head, feel the bumps in the middle of the back of her neck. These are the spinous processes of the vertebrae. If pushing gently on any of these hurts, you have to assume the neck is broken until checked out by an X ray. Even a little tenderness is suspect! If there's no tenderness at all, and she's totally awake and with it, and has no pain at all with any kind of motion of her neck, you can assume her neck is OK enough to move her.

Check the Head and Chest

Feel the bones in her face, looking for tenderness. Ask her to open her mouth (the normal opening between the top and bottom teeth in front is 35mm.) If she can't open all the way, that's suspect. Feel her Adam's apple to make sure it's in the middle. Push down on the front of her chest when she takes a deep breath, and then squeeze the sides of her rib cage while she takes another deep breath. Broken ribs will hurt.

Check the Abdomen

Mash gently all around the belly, looking for tenderness or unusual tightness (or "guarding").

Check the Limbs

Squeeze the hipbones together and push down on the pubic bone, looking for pain. Roll each leg back and forth; bend each knee all the way; twist each ankle; and squeeze along each foot.

Ask her to put her hands straight out in front of her face; then roll her fists in a circle; touch each of her fingers with the thumb of the same hand; put her hands on her shoulders; and move her elbows in a big circle. Last (assuming the neck is OK and her back doesn't hurt) have her roll sideways and gently pound down the backbone with your fist. Then hit softly over each kidney, just below where the ribs join the backbone.

If any of the above maneuvers causes pain, it's worth having it checked out at your local emergency room or by your own doc. Any neck, chest, head or belly pain should be checked right away—and in fact, it would be reasonable to call an ambulance to transport somebody with pain in one of those areas. If an arm, leg, hand or foot is apparently broken, (doesn't work or look right) have that checked right away, also. Any cuts present should be washed with soap and water, if possible; covered with a clean (preferably sterile) dressing, and checked to see if they need to be stitched. If so, you have a MAXI-MUM of six hours to do so for most cuts—otherwise, there are too many germs already growing in the wound to suture it. It's best to have it looked at right away. And don't forget to ask if you need a tetanus shot—they're good for five to ten years.

And please, don't be foolish and decide you can best carry your friend with the possible broken neck on the back of your bike to the emergency room to be seen. You could cause real harm. Doing something like that reminds me of the woman I saw in an emergency room who drove her husband to the hospital in their car, while he was having an obvious heart attack. "Why," I said "didn't you just call nine-eleven for an ambulance?" "Well, I meant to," she replied "but I couldn't find the eleven on the telephone . . . "

Care and Treatment

Don't Be Stupid

Ya Gotta Have Heart

Coronary artery disease kills about half a million people a year. Most of the deaths from this problem are sudden. If you don't recognize the early symptoms of coronary artery disease, the sudden death could be yours. Statistically, you're a lot more likely to die of heart disease than a motorcycle accident.

Chest pain is always a worrisome symptom. When I was working in emergency rooms, a patient with chest pain always got priority, since those patients had a tendency to keel over without warning. When somebody's heart stops in a hospital, it's sometimes called a "code blue." Folks working in the E.R. didn't like to do code blues on people, especially around meal time or change of shift. You're a lot better off just staying healthy in the first place.

You can have coronary artery disease at almost any age. I remember, for example, an 18 year-old woman who was in the E.R. at Jackson Memorial Hospital in Miami, Florida, when I was in training there. She kept clutching her chest and saying "I'm dyin'! I'm dyin'!!" Though she wasn't at much risk for a heart attack at that age, the resident went ahead and got an EKG (electrocardiogram) on her anyhow. It was normal, and he told her to just relax. (He may have thought she was hysterical). She had a cardiac arrest less than a minute after that and couldn't be resuscitated. Her autopsy showed several *old* heart attacks in addition to the new one that had killed her.

The first heart surgery for coronary artery disease I had myself was a technique called an

Death

Chest Pain

Youth is Not Immunity

Surgery

95

"angioplasty." It's kind of like using a real small Roto-Rooter on the heart's own arteries. With luck, it'll clear the blockage and in a few days you'll be better. Occasionally, though, it doesn't work or the cardiologist doing it messes up and you need emergency open heart surgery. Luckily, all six that I have had worked pretty well.

Even though there are some pretty good techniques for opening up arteries, they won't do you any good if you die before you get to the hospital, as two thirds of all folks who die suddenly of coronary artery disease (C.A.D.) do. Since many folks get symptoms of a heart attack before their hearts stop, it's worth knowing what to watch for.

Heart Attack Symptoms

The classic symptoms of a heart attack are chest pain (sometimes felt only as pressure) usually in the middle or slightly to the left of the middle of the chest; shortness of breath; sweating; and often nausea. People often complain of pain going down the left arm. Though people can get heart attacks while exerting themselves (say, by trying to turn a dirt bike around on the side of a hill) they can also be caused by a big meal or by emotional upset ("Mr. Jones?" "Yes, doctor?" "We've got your tests back. You've got a very weak heart. The slightest shock could kill you. Mr. Jones? Mr. Jones??" [THUD]).

Pain, or No Pain

The pain from a heart attack isn't overwhelming in many cases. It's possible to have a heart attack with only some aching, heartburn, "upset stomach," gas, or other non-specific kinds of discomfort. Older folks can have heart attacks without even having the usual symptoms! Classically, people feel a dull, heavy pressure on their chest along with the queasiness; they also usually feel hot, sweaty, or clammy. Often, there's pain in the left arm, or sometimes in the jaw.

High Blood Pressure

How can you prevent heart attacks? High blood pressure is a major risk factor for C.A.D. Contrary to what many people believe, you don't usually feel high blood pressure. I recommend that you get your blood pressure checked regularly, whenever the opportunity presents itself. Some emergency rooms and urgent care centers will check your pressure for you without charge: just call and ask first. New medications now available for hypertension (which has NOTHING to do with how "tense" you are) have fewer side effects than ever.

Every time your heart beats, pushing blood against a high arterial resistance (which causes high blood pressure), it has to work harder. In working harder, the heart muscle itself gets thicker. This might be nice for biceps, but not for your heart. Since blood supplies the heart only from the outside, the thicker the heart muscle, the farther the blood has to go to get all the way through it. The farther it goes, the greater chance for a blockage, or, in other words, a heart attack.

Cholesterol

High cholesterol levels are another risk factor. It's well worth knowing what yours is, especially if you have a family history of heart attacks or strokes. If you get it checked, be sure your doctor tells you how much of your cholesterol is "good" (i.e., high density) versus "bad" (low density).

Heredity

Family history's important, too. You need to choose your ancestors carefully if you plan to live forever. A strong history of heart attacks ought to make you careful about things that you can do something about, like cholesterol, blood pressure, and cigarette smoking.

Risk Factors

Other less important risk factors are obesity, lack of exercise, and stress. If you are already at increased risk because of diabetes, prior MI (myocardial infarction, or heart attack), or a strong family history of premature cardiovascular disease, you really need to be aware of things like your cholesterol and your blood pressure.

Smoking

A big risk factor is cigarette smoking. Tobacco smoke lowers the oxygen-carrying capability of your blood, which starves your heart for oxygen. Cigarettes cause lung damage, too, which then chronically suffocates your body, heart, and brain. It's been estimated that one out of ten Americans alive today will die prematurely from cigarette smoking and that many of those deaths will be sudden (and that's one out of ten Americans—*not* one out of ten smokers!). Since about three out of ten Americans smoke,

97

that translates to one out of three smokers who'll die prematurely—which is about the same odds as you'll get playing Russian roulette.

Bang!

    With two bullets . . .

These Boots Are Made For . . .

They shoot horses, don't they? At least, they make movies with that title. I know the feeling you get when you have to put a trusted, faithful companion out of its misery.

I feel like that about my old boots. They're more than just bike boots: I wore 'em every place for the past dozen years. They're Frye's, with the zipper down the inside. They have squared-off heels. Big, wide toes. After all these years, and after four or five new soles, they were getting just about right. They've even learned to come crawling over to the bed in the morning.

Well, I took them in for repairs, and the cobbler had difficulty not laughing. "These boots have more holes than Albert Hall! They're worn through the shift lever patch over the left toe. They have three holes big enough to put a finger through!! What is it about this pair: sentimental value?"

I guess that's what it is. Usually, I try not to get attached to "things"—they're too ephemeral. Like they say: here today, gone to Maui. These boots, though, are different. I wore 'em in 1980 when I rode from San Francisco to Boston. It was a nice trip. I wore the boots.

When I got to Boston, I had a surprise waiting from the moving company. They wrote:

"Dear Dr. Gordon: You had certain goods in storage in our Randolph, Massachusetts warehouse awaiting your arrival. Unfortunately, this facility was totally destroyed by fire on July 26th. Please complete the enclosed claim forms, listing every item, its cost when new, cost of replacement, date of purchase, and attach receipts. . ."

Loving Old Boots

99

Well, after getting the moving company's check, my furniture looks like I have good taste. My towels even match, so it wasn't all bad. My boots were OK. You can see why I'm attached to them. But today, something happened.

I was down at Bavarian Cycle Works in San Francisco getting a fuse, and decided (on general principles) to see what was new in the world of riding footwear. "Try the 'moon boots,' " they said. "Not only . . .

Quake!!!

[WOW—just had a good aftershock while typing this. In fact, we've had so much earthquake activity that I've started telling patients that if they REALLY want to have safe sex, they should do it in a doorway. . .]

". . . Try the 'moon boots,' " they said. "Not only are they comfortable, you get a perfect feel of the machine's foot controls. You can judge your brake pressure perfectly."

"I feel it just fine with these old Frye's," I scoffed.

They insisted, nicely. "Try a pair. Sit on the machine."

And Then There's the New Boots . . .

I unzipped my old buddies and tried the 'moon boots.' Strange. No heel, just a flush sole. They weighed less, too. Plenty of sideways crush resistance. After crushing some bones in my left foot in 1962 in high school while riding with sneakers, I think crush resistance is essential. The new boots had lots of flex, too. They felt like a leather running shoe going to mid-calf.

Still, I've got sales resistance, except when it comes to macadamia nuts (that's another story). No impulse buying for me. Before buying anything as major as new boots, I'd probably go to Barney's in San Rafael; Marin Cycle; hit California BMW in Mountain View, and probably San Jose BMW (I'm not a shopper: I'm a careful consumer).

"Sorry—not today," I replied. I started to put on my old boots, and, for the first time in their dozen or so years, the zipper on the left boot jammed. Shit. I grabbed the pull with my little folding Leatherman tool pliers, and the zipper started dropping teeth like a tree shedding leaves in the fall . . .

Actually, these new boots aren't bad. In fact, I think I'll get an extra pair. Strictly as a back-up, you understand. I believe in redundancy. I believe in re-dundancy.

You Need This
Like a Hole in the Head

Question: How are your sinuses and a motorcycle helmet liner alike?

Answer: They both are designed to protect your brain by crumpling on impact.

Question: How are your sinuses and a motorcycle helmet liner different?

Answer: When your helmet liner gives you problems, you can get a new helmet. When your sinuses act up, you're stuck with them.

Your sinuses are in your face. You've got a pair under your eyes in your cheeks; a pair just behind the bridge of your nose; and a pair in your forehead above your eyes. If you put your hands flat over your face, they'll cover all your sinuses.

Where Are They?

When the bones of the face form, there are spaces left in the bone. All these spaces have a tiny opening into your nose, way high up. They do have a purpose above and beyond providing reasons for patients to visit doctors—they make the skull lighter; they help your voice resonate; and, importantly, provide a "crumple zone" that can protect your brain. When your face hits something (or something hits you) very hard, the sinuses break first, absorbing some of the impact and (hopefully) preventing lethal damage.

How They Work

Sinuses are lined with the same kind of skin that's inside the nose and lungs. These cells produce mucus (which is designed to catch dust and germs, like flypaper) and sweep the mucus to the sinus opening, which is about as big as this letter "O."

Flypaper

Facial Structure

People's sinus openings vary in size. People with long, narrow faces have more sinus problems—that is, people with the "Prince Charles" type face. People with wide faces like Nanook of the North don't get as much sinus trouble.

Blockage

Sinuses get blocked when the mucus doesn't drain as fast as it's produced. Anything that causes your nose to run probably causes your sinuses to make more mucus, too. Allergies can do it, as can a cold or even chronic exposure to irritants. If the sinuses aren't able to empty themselves through the tiny hole to the nose, you've got a problem.

Allergies

If allergies are your problem, there are now some new allergy treatments that can really help. Newer drugs available by prescription don't make you sleepy, and there are topical steroid nasal sprays that can eliminate allergy symptoms in many people.

Drainage Problems

Two factors really impair the ability of the sinuses to drain—tobacco smoke and dryness. The nicotine in tobacco paralyzes the cells that sweep out the dust and germ-laden mucus, and dryness makes it harder and stickier. If you've ever spent time outside in a very hot and dry place, you know what it can do to the mucus in your nose—it turns dry, hard, and sticky. Your sinuses are designed to move moist, liquid mucus, not rocks.

Blockage Makes Pressure Which Makes Pain and Infection

The problems get worse quickly if the opening to the sinus is blocked by one of these chunks of dried mucus. The cells that produce mucus keep on doing so, even when the sinus isn't draining normally. This increases pressure, and pressure causes pain. Also, once you've got a pool of stagnant mucus in your sinus, it's ripe for infection. There's nothing more appetizing to a germ than a pool of stagnant mucus. Yum!

Big Trouble

Once your sinus is infected, the real trouble starts. If the pressure gets high enough, it impairs the blood flow to the skin lining the sinus, and the body isn't able to get white blood cells into the area to fight the infection. The germs then grow unopposed, and you can find yourself in a serious predicament. People can die from bad sinus infections that don't get proper treatment.

When the sinus is badly infected, it'll hurt. It will be tender if you tap on the forehead or face over the sinus; the skin may be warm or red; and often you'll have a fever. This is a medical emergency: you should see a doctor without delay. When a sinus gets a bacterial infection, antibiotics can be life-saving.

See a Doctor

Two things are necessary in treatment: drain the sinus, and kill the germs. Of the two, drainage is the most important. Remember the dried mucus that can plug the sinus opening? This may be contributing to the problem. To moisten it, you must drink lots of extra fluids (try to drink enough to make your urine clear) and get more moisture in the air you're breathing. Taking a hot shower and closing the doors and windows with the fan off can help; so can putting your face over a steaming hot pan of water with a towel over your head. If you can moisten a piece of dried mucus that's blocking the tiny sinus opening, you might make it slippery enough to slip out.

Drinking & Getting Steamed

Other factors that contribute to blocking the sinuses include swollen mucus membranes. If your nose is stuffy and it's hard to breath, chances are the opening to your sinuses are swollen and it's hard for them to drain. One of the few times that I recommend decongestants is when a sinus is blocked. If you do take them, take extra fluids! I also recommend a 12-hour nasal spray (most brands are the same) to shrink swollen membranes.

Decongestants

It's important to use nasal sprays correctly. First, try not to use them for more than about five days, or you might get rebound congestion when you stop. When actually using the spray, you need to decongest your nose all the way up to the sinus opening. Since your nose has two little "shelves" of bone (called turbinates) that make the air you breath swirl and drop its dust on the lining, you must decongest it a stage at a time.

Mastering Nasal Sprays

Blow your nose well, and clean out whatever you can. Then, close the other nostril with a finger; breath in sharply and spray the decongestant into each nostril; wait three minutes; repeat; wait three minutes; repeat a third time. This will hopefully open your nose all the way back to the sinus opening, and the decongestant may shrink the tissues around the hole itself, hopefully relieving the blockage.

Draining your Face

Once your nose is open, it would be a good time to breath in the steam I mentioned earlier. Also, if one side of your face is more congested than the other, sleep with the bad side up. It's easier for a sinus to drain downhill. Some people find a hot water bottle or heating pad helps, too.

One Last Smoking Warning . . .

Remember: tobacco smoke paralyzes your sinus linings, as well as your lungs. People need cigarettes like a hole in the head, too.

Index

helmets 11, 29, 39, 70, 103
  hearing with 50
hemorrhoids 65–67
heredity 97
heroin 59
high blood pressure 83–85, 96–97
Hippo Hands 73
Hitler 8
honeymoon paralysis 37
hydrogen peroxide 18
hypertension 97
hypothermia 70–73

I

ibuprofen 31, 34, 42, 45, 47, 66
ice 15, 17–18, 42
Imodium 53
indigestion 51
infection 22, 57
  poison oak 26
  sinus 104–105
influenza 59
injuries 8, 19, 21
  See also wounds, burns
Internet vi
iodine 13, 17
  See also disinfectant
irritants 104
itching 26

J

Jiminy Cricket 78
juices 53

K

Kaopectate 52
Kenalog 26
Kerlix gauze bandages 88

L

L.L. Bean 73
leather 7, 71
legs
  broken 93
  pain, numbness, and weakness 47
letter to yourself 83–84
Life Savers 79
ligaments 41
Lomotil 52–53
long johns 73
lungs 59, 106

M

Maalox 52
macadamia nuts 100
magic 84
massage 45–46
Maui 99
Meaning of Life, The 51
memory loss 81
menopause 81
Mercurochrome 13
Metamucil 66–67
Metzeler 70
Micatin 57
Mickey Mouse 78
miconazole 57
motoholics 63
mucus 103–104
mucus membranes, swelling 105
muscle spasms 46
muscles 41, 84
Mussolini 8

N

Nanook of the North 104
Napoleon 8, 65
Naproxen 42, 45, 47
narcotics 52
nasal sprays 104–105
nausea 53, 96
neck
  broken 38, 88, 91
  pain 92
needle 17
Neosporin 15
nerves 33, 37
  pinched 37–38
nicotine 104
noise 49
nose 103–106
numbness
  hands 33, 38
  legs 47
  wrists 34

O

obesity 97
osteoporosis 81–82

tobacco
  See smoking
toenail, blue 57
toes 55, 57
  broken 55
  buddy-taping 55
traction 69
trauma check 88, 91–93
trauma, repetitive 33, 41
travel 52
trees 25
Tums 52
tweezers 22
Tylenol 34, 42, 61
Type A personalities 77–79

U

Ulmer, Diane, R.N., M.S. 78–79
unconditional love 77
undershirts, silk long-sleeved 73
upset stomach 52, 96
urine 61, 105

V

veins, hemorrhoidal 65
vest, electric 73

viruses 59
  See also bacteria
visibility 69
vision 11, 30
vomiting 51, 53

W

Waterloo, Battle of 65
weakness
  hands 33
  leg 47
weight 84–85
weight transfer 9
wheezing 61
Whole Earth Review vi
windchill factor 7, 72
windscreens 29
wounds 17
  See also injuries
wrists 33–35

X

X rays 55, 92
Xylocaine 18, 66

Z

zinc oxide 16, 18, 23, 57
zipper 99–100